Conten

C000140168

Volume 96:3 Autumn 2006

Poems

4	Sean O'Brien	from Canto XXVI Of *The Inferno* Of Dante Alighieri
7	Robin Robertson	after Tranströmer: Winter's Code
		Sketch In October
		From March 1979
10	Eavan Boland	An Elegy For My Mother In Which She Scarcely Appears
12	Peter Porter	On The Best Battlefields No Dead Bodies
13	John Kinsella	from *Purgatorio: Up Close:*
		Canto Of Declamatory Players
		Canto Apostrophe
		Dream Canto 8 – Recurring:
		Doodenanning Golf Course
18	David Morley	Songs Of Songs
20	Greg Delanty	The Wordmen
21	Mimi Khalvati	Sundays
24	Tim Liardet	from North Of Everything
28	Steven Matthews	from Essex Coastal
29	Andrew Motion	A1 Mechanics
30	David Harsent	after Cavafy: The Art Of Poetry
		At The Tobacconist's Window
		Afternoon Sun
32	Greta Stoddart	Instrument
33	Allison Funk	Penelope At Home
35	Mohammad Hoghughi	All With Wings
36	Nazand Begikhani	Calm
37	Fred Voss	Starting The Avalanche
39	Peter McDonald	Against The Fear Of Death
40	Mustafa Stitou	Coffin
41	Pascale Petit	Atlas Moth
42	A A Marcoff	The Hymn Of The Radiant
45	Jane Holland	Books At Auction

Conversation: Fish and Bicycle

48	Gagan Gill	Fish
49	Susan Wicks	Cycling To See The Fish-Ladder

50	Andrew Johnston	The Cyclist
51	Judith Kazantzis	The Dose
52	Kelly Grovier	Rain, Steam, And Speed
53	Michael Schmidt	Pangur Bàn

Centrefold

56	John Burnside	*Mind the Gap: On Reading American Poetry*
68	Don Paterson	*Aphorisms*
70	Hélène Cixous	from *Manhattan*

"Representative Writing"…?

78	Daljit Nagra	My Father's Dream Of Return
80	Saradha Soobrayen	As I Am
81	E. A. Markham	*from* At Home With Miss Vanesa
82	Patience Agbabi	*from* Problem Pages
84	Parm Kaur	Notes For A Debate On Identity And Representative Publishing
85	Eva Salzman	Under The Radar
86	Satish Kumar	Representing The Landscape
88	Menna Elfyn	Libanus, Y Pwll
90	Bernardine Evaristo	Mixing Up The Metaphors

Reviews

92	David Morley on Charles Tomlinson, Peter Redgrove, Philip Gross and Greg Delanty
95	Elaine Feinstein on Eavan Boland and Muriel Spark
98	Matthew Jarvis on Simon Armitage
100	Michelene Wandor on Vicki Feaver, Selima Hill and Grace Nichols
103	William Palmer on Ruth Fainlight
105	Paul Batchelor on Penelope Shuttle
108	George Szirtes on John Haynes and Tim Liardet
111	Kit Fan on Chase Twichell, Elizabeth Alexander and Tomaž Šalamun
114	Judith Kazantzis on Michelene Wandor, Imtiaz Dharker, Janet Sutherland and Helen Ivory
117	Nigel McLoughlin's small press round-up
121	Stephen Knight on Kate Bingham, Tishani Doshi and Jenny Joseph

Endpapers

126	Chase Twichell	*Letter from The Adirondacks*
127	Editorial	
128	Contributors	

POEMS

⅋

Beautiful, grave world.
—Andrew Motion

Sean O'Brien
from Canto XXVI Of The Inferno
Of Dante Alighieri

Dante and Virgil encounter Ulysses

We waited. When the flame had reached the place
And time my leader thought most suitable,
I heard him speaking to its prisoners thus:

'O you who form a pair within one flame,
If I gained merit with you while I lived,
If I earned much or little gratitude

For those great lines I wrote when in the world,
Then do not go, but let one of you speak
Of where he went, when lost, to meet his death.'

At this the ancient fire's taller half
Began to murmur, shuddering as though
It cowered from the scourging of the wind.

Then flickering its tip this way and that
As if it were a tongue that spoke, the flame
Threw out a voice, which said: 'When I escaped

From Circe, who had held me there a year
Near Gaeta – which great Aeneas named –
Then neither my affection for my son,

Nor reverence for my aged father, nor
The love I owed towards Penelope,
Which should at last have sealed her happiness,

Could quench the longing that I bore: to gain
Experience of the world, and of the kinds
Of human vice and virtue it contained.

But I set out upon the open deep
With one small vessel only and those few
Old crewmen who had not deserted me.

I saw the shores to north and south as far
As Spain, Morocco and Sardinia
And other isles that sea encompasses.

My company and I were old and slow
When finally we reached that narrow strait
Where Hercules had set his markers up

In order that no man should pass beyond.
To starboard I had left Seville; to port
Ceuta had already slipped behind.

"My brothers," I said then, "we reach the west
Despite a hundred thousand dangers. Now
Let us not deny ourselves experience –

In this, the last watch that remains to us
To know – of going on, beyond the sun,
Into the world in which no human lives.

Reflect upon your origins: such men
Were never born to live their lives as brutes,
But go in search of virtue and the truth."

And with this little speech I made my crew
So ardent for the voyage now at hand,
I did not have the power to hold them back.

We turned our stern towards the morning then,
And gaining always on the larboard side
We made our oars the wings of that wild flight.

The night now saw the southern pole and stars.
Meanwhile, the skies of home had sunk so low
They never broke the surface of the deep.

Five times we saw the moon rekindling,
Five times we saw it quenched since we embarked
Upon our crossing of that sea, and then

Before us there appeared a mountain, dark
And distant, which it seemed to me must be
The highest I had ever seen. At this

We all rejoiced, but soon our joy was turned
To grief, for out of this new land there rose
A whirlwind which then struck us at the bow.

Three times it whirled us in a waterspout
And on the fourth it raised the stern aloft
And plunged the prow beneath the waves, as pleased

Another, till the sea closed over us.'

Robin Robertson
after Tranströmer

Winter's Code

1.

I fell asleep in my bed
and woke up under the keel.

At four in the morning
life's clean-picked bones
engage in brittle repartee.

I fell asleep among the swallows
and woke among eagles.

2.

In the lamplight the ice on the road
gleams like glycerine.

This is not Africa.
This is not Europe.
This is nowhere else but 'here'.

And that which was 'I'
is only a word
in the darkness of December's mouth.

3.

The asylum pavilions,
lit up in the night,
are bright as TV screens.

A hidden tuning-fork
in the great cold
throws out its shivering tone.

I stand under the starry sky
and feel the world thrill
through me, like the pulse
of ants in an anthill.

4.

Three black oaks rear through the snow:
rough, but nimble-fingered.
In the spring, their giant bottles
will froth with green.

5.

The bus negotiates the winter night:
a flickering ship in the pine forest
on a road as narrow and deep as a dead canal.

Few passengers: some old, some very young.
If it stopped and switched off its lights
the world would be deleted.

Sketch In October

The tugboat is freckled with rust. What is it doing so far inland?
It's a heavy burnt-out lamp, tipped over in the cold.
But the trees still carry colours – wild signals to the other shore as if
someone wanted to be fetched home.

On the way back, I see mushrooms pushing up through the grass.
Stretching for help, these white fingers
belong to someone who sobs down there in the darkness.
We belong to the earth.

From March 1979

Sick of those who come with words, words but no language,
I make my way to the snow-covered island.

Wilderness has no words. The unwritten pages
stretch out in all directions.

I come across this line of deer-slots in the snow: a language,
language without words.

Eavan Boland
An Elegy For My Mother In Which She Scarcely Appears

I knew we had to grieve for the animals
a long time ago: weep for them, pity them.
I knew it was our strange human duty
to write their elegies after we arranged their demise.
I was young then and able for the paradox.
I am older now and ready with the question:
What happened to them all? I mean to those
old dumb implements which have
no eyes to plead with us like theirs,
no claim to make on us like theirs? I mean –

there was a singing kettle. I want to know
why no one tagged its neck or ringed the tin
base of its extinct design or crouched to hear
its rising shriek in winter or wrote it down with
the birds in their blue sleeves of air
torn away with the trees that sheltered them.

And there were brass fire dogs which lay out
all evening on the grate and in the heat
thrown at them by the last of the peat fire
but no one noted down their history or put them
in the old packs under slate-blue moonlight.
There was a wooden clothes-horse, absolutely steady
without sinews, with no mane and no meadows
to canter in; carrying, instead of
landlords or Irish monks, rinsed tea cloths
but still, I would have thought, worth adding to
the catalogue of what we need, what we always need

as is my mother, on this Dublin evening of
fog crystals and frost as she reaches out to test
one corner of a cloth for dryness as the pre-war
Irish twilight closes in and down on the room
and the curtains are drawn and here am I,
not even born and already a conservationist,
with nothing to assist me but the last
and most fabulous of beasts – language, language –
which knows, as I do, that it's too late
to record the loss of these things but does so anyway,
and anxiously, in case it shares their fate.

Peter Porter
On The Best Battlefields
No Dead Bodies*

Death is unfit for anything but writing about.
On *The Antiques Road Show* it adopts the posture
of an Eighteenth Century culverin
which should be insured for Fifteen Hundred Pounds
and still we know how much it costs to cast
a trainee pilot in a jet into the Irish Sea.
It is happily content to be
'the trigger of the Literary Man's biggest gun',
hating, as it does, both noise and smells,
and bikes to work masked like a Tokyo commuter.
Itself its favourite word, it is as politic
as Faith and lets statistics arabesque
those glaciers that melt and birds which leave their eggs;
it is in perfect taste even for an Age
which has no taste –
                    touch it as you touch yourself
in commentary or horror – there's nothing there.
Superior to rhyme, it lives in poems
'that will never die.'
                    It says, a lover of quotation,
its glory is it had such friends
and a refrigerated Heaven to retire to.
And now the Poet tells what might be true –
she was made a legatee of battlefields,
of every pibroch and retreat across the years
and affirms that no-one dies,
no word or ward is lost –
instead, and scattered round,
all that she sees is offered to the gods,
the hasty permanence of sanity.

*From Veronica Forrest-Thomson's 'Lemon and Rosemary'.

John Kinsella
from *Purgatorio: Up Close*

Canto Of Declamatory Players

Who describes where we are without thinking
of when we'll leave it? Declamatory players,
wasps rebuilding, mosquitoes emerging

where there's no oil upon waters: bite on bite
driving you back in behind flywire, night sky
anathema, star wheel locked in its carded sleeve.

Events, you force to order: unbalanced wheel
that wears heavily on inmost orbit of tyre,
a tremor in steerage, constant correcting

to keep it going towards the mountain.
A double flight of tawny frogmouths:
cryptic colouration so still on a day-lit branch,

they transfigure, overlooked to await the negative:
and yet, in sharply diffused paradox of high beam,
they are bright angels driving off a snake

that sleeps at night, coiled about the core.
What takes the ants from their bare empire
out on trails of trade and exploration,

to spend months scouring one eucalypt
and to leave it just as suddenly, pathway
smooth through stubble neglected,

closing over, others to younger eucalypts
opened up and polished through travel in no time?
So, we watch the ants. Trace minute heat signatures

in a realm of heat. So, double-struck by lightning,
I wait half anxious and half inviting the next strike,
clouds cloistering, grinding to draw static

out of rocks and dirt, illuminate water.
And Stephen, planting trees to close us in,
all others out; or, looking past hills, inland,

thinking of oceans, waves that keep him under,
under-currents that churn him over and over.
And Katherine, surrounding the house,

rapping at the shutters crying through the locks.
And John, building, building, building,
keeping the elements out, making shelter.

And Wendy, negotiating with neighbours,
wondering why here is no better than anywhere else.
And Tracy, wondering in other languages,

writing elegies, reliving her births. And Timmy,
counting, singing, tapping out a tune to the full moon,
the "beautiful mountain" covered in cloud.

Before long grass is cut, you can follow
swirls and counter-swirls of willy-willy paths:
different and collusive narratives, often

moving counter-clockwise, against the clock.
In that small tornado's time, Katherine and her
friend Zoë make up, and sell their hand-crafted

jewellery at York's once-a-month Saturday markets,
a five-dollar stall that contributes to a fund
for the starving in Africa: here, donations are generic

to many, but they don't mind making one.
Hearing music – the drums from Stephen's room –
I leave the car, headlights off, to glower under stars,

here music that's heaven, hell, and purgatory
rolled into one: what other way is there here
where all "kingdoms" are one and none.

ℬ

Canto Apostrophes

You, mouse in the atrium, runner
of wall cavities, traverser of steel frame
between brick and gyprock,

immiscible singer of endless nightmare,
as right as rain, as up and Adam,
as trawling the depths;

asserting additive territory,
who skip in from outside
broad field in moonlight

laden with seed? Composing
mateship and courtship rituals
not yet tested for? You, subdivisions,

to draft clean air bills
in roof cavity, or knock down
chicken-wire inflection

where fowl are no longer,
common fence with unmade
roadway, terrace shifting tense?

Or driving out, past crow
and blazon feather of Port Lincoln,
wing feather attributing wobble

in solar exposition: going back
down the hill, about-facing
the long trek to estuarine water,

boats lever-arching out
of each wake, to clatter
mast against means and agent.

Stray dogs, pack sheep,
ponies, alpacas, against the fence,
and pink and greys

conserving interests: intense
on mowed green tint,
hooking seeds that won't sprout.

ॐ

Dream Canto 8 – Recurring: Doodenanning Golf Course

Swear it has been dreamt before? Same steps
out on the golf course, the layers of oil and dirt,
jam trees and deformed wandoos with termite-

hollowed limbs like ventricles of the heart?
The second nine stretched out through salt scald?
But there's vegetation missing: grasses, acacia

saplings... more than lost to the *second driest Autumn*
on record. Records. Every year, more records.
You dream of it as Timmy dreams orange juice,

orange sky, orange soil, orange trees, the mountain
as orange. Here, it's a thin carpet of ash and char,
a burning off to keep the fairways and rough

"manageable"... the roos up against the fences
with no feed where feed was already thin,
and families down by the tennis courts

chopping deadwood with a chainsaw,
something religious about them, something
like a church group out for the long weekend,

playing tennis, indifferent to golf: calling
out to us as we step out: *strangers strangers strangers,*
out here beyond the shire's circulatory system:

what business do they have here? Why do they
walk the course, looking at pink and greys
and analysing the droppings of marsupials:
outside the game, outside the discourse?

David Morley
Songs Of Songs

A Romani version

I am black, but comely, O ye daughters of Jerusalem, as the
katòoni of Kedar, as the perdès of Solomon.

I have compared thee, O mi dèhiba, to chatimè gras in Pharaoh's
vardos.

For while the king beshàv at his sharibè, my spikenard sendeth
forth the soong thereof.

Behold, thou art lacshòo, mi dèhiba; behold, thou art lacshòo,
thou hast goorgoorìtsa yakh.

For I am the rose of Sharon, and the parnò looloodì of the har.

As the parnò looloodì among karòs, so is mi dèhiba among her
cshays.

Stay me with flagons, comfort me with aphai: for I am nasvalòo
of kamav.

For I charge you, o ye cshays of Jerusalem, by the surnà, and by
the surnà of the oomalyàkom, that ye stir not up, nor awake
mi dèhiba, till mangàva.

---

katòoni: tents; **perdès:** curtain; **mi dèhiba:** my love, my beloved; **chatimè gras:** a
company of horse assembled; **Pharaoh** or **Firaòni:** the Gypsy King of the Gypsy fairy
tales or 'paramisi'; **vardos:** wagons; **beshàv:** sits; **sharibè:** table; **soong:** smell; **lacshòo:**
fair, handsome; **goorgoorìtsa yakh:** dove's eyes; **parnò looloodì:** white flower [lily];
har: valley; **karòs:** thorns, stings (n); **cshays:** daughters; **aphai:** apples; **nasvalòo:** sick;
kamav: love; **surnà:** deer; **oomalyàkom:** field; **mangàva:** wishes, pleases.

Looloodì appear on the doonyàs, the tsìros of chiriklògìlyaiba is come, and the sèsi of the goorgoorìtsa is heard in our phoov.

Take us to the weshjooks, the tsikooroo weshjooks, that spoil the vitsa: for amarò vitsa have parus drakhà.

Until sabàlen, and the oochipè flees away, ìrin, mi dèhiba, and be thou like a roe or a ternò surnà upon the plàyna of Bether.

I will rise now, and go about the fòros in the òolitsa, and in the boohlò putèka I will seek him, my ozì piryamlòo: I sought him, amà I found him not.

Avàv from Lebanon, my rom, avàv from Lebanon: dikhav from the hip of Amana, from the hip of Shenir and Hermon, from the dens of aslàni, from the plàyna of leopards.

Ko adavkhà that cometh out of the wilderness like pillars of thoov, smelling of myrrh and frankincense, with all powders of the Roma?

Spikenard and saffron; calamus and cinnamon, with all trees of frankincense; myrrh and aloes, with sòvra spices.

For King Solomon has made himself a vardo of the kash of Lebanon.

---

looloodì: flowers; doonyàs: earth; tsìros: time; chiriklògìlyaiba: singing of birds; sèsi: voice; goorgoorìtsa: dove; phoov: land; weshjooks: foxes; tsikooroo weshjooks: little foxes; vitsa: vine; amarò: our; parus: soft; drakhà: grapes; sabàlen: daybreak; oochipè: shadow; ìrin: turn around; ternò surnà: young deer; plàyna: mountain; fòros: city; òolitsa: streets; boohlò: broad; putèka: paths; ozì piryamlòo: soul's lover; amà: but; avàv: come (imp); rom: husband, spouse; dikhav: look; hip: top; aslàni: lions; ko adavkhà: who is this; thoov: smoke; Roma: gypsy [travelling merchant]; sòvra: all; vardo: wagon; kash: wood.

Greg Delanty
The Wordmen

It's not impossible that from the very start
    I've been at something akin to
        what the Dogon buckoos do:
how they mussitate extended tales by heart
of the gene-myths of their ancestors into
their women's auricles. And it's these seed-words
        they say – after they enter
    the meatus of the ear and spiral downwards
past the throat and through the proofing liver
    before doing a whirly around the venter
        and settling with a word quiver –
that set the composed woman in the family way.
Incorrect as it is, fantabulous as it sounds, to us,
    it's no more unbelievable, my lovely lay,
than the fetus pressed like an ear to your uterus.

Mimi Khalvati
Sundays

for Tom

i.

Together, we have made sour cherry rice,
rolled minced lamb into meatballs and listened
to the radio while eating, him to stall
hallucinations and me to respect his silence,

the time he takes to eat. We've strolled slowly
in the park together, our favourite park,
lapsing into pauses with the falling light –
tennis in the distance – as we slowly climbed

the hill. I've left my shoes at the door, him
reminding me, to scrub off the dogshit later
and now he's at the piano in the nowhere hour
before TV. These are the things that make him

well – company, old and easy, recipes
old but new to him. His playing brings
the night in. Turns the streetlamps on, makes
the kitchen clock tick. Softly a chord falls

and out of the ground grow snowdrops, fat and waxy
with green hearts, upside down, stamped beneath
white aprons, poking their heads through railings.
Between his fingers things grow, little demons,

fountains, crocuses. Spring is announced and enters,
one long green glove unfingering the other,
icicles melt and rivers run, bluetits
hop and trill. Everything talks to everything.

ii.

Oh it poured with rain today. My gutter,
blocked and inaccessible to anyone bar
the man with the longest ladder in London,
waterfalled down the window alarmingly.

No, the waterfall is here, under his fingers,
steady wrists, the years of training paying off
in instinctual music; and the fat raindrops, spraying
up like diamanté; and the tailing off

of rain, all the languages of rain, rivers,
gutters, waterfalls, the treble runs
of rain and the bass's percussive beat;
all the liquidity of youth, youth gone

to rack and ruin. How little he ate today
and how much there was to eat – stuffed pepper,
salmon, apple and blackberry tart, coffee.
He can't even swallow his own saliva,

holding it in his mouth minutes at a time,
without hearing them, the voices, seeing
babies streaming towards his mouth, limbs
trigger words command him: that, there, take, eat.

iii.

He ate all of it. All of the rice
and all of the *khoreshté bademjan*
– the aubergine dish – I carefully filled
his plate with, not overfilled. He liked it.

He was always sweet about my cooking.
We ate while watching *West Side Story*.
How easy it was to sorrow for Maria
and Tony. Easy to cry and grieve.

Now he's at the piano, today
so tentative, but gaining in assurance
like someone 'learning to live with disability'.
Is he? Or is that someone me?

all of us, all of us who love him.
Joey rings. He's free tomorrow,
Tom's saying – he hasn't decided yet
whether to stay with me a while,

I hope he will. And suddenly
there's sunshine, brightness and a bounce
and his fingers are dancing. Voices
might bedevil him but voices also

save him – Moss's, Joey's, Sara's –
or let him down without meaning to,
without knowing, after they've finished
a call, the music stops again

as suddenly as it started. But now
he's into it – and what's that tune?
coming and going. Tom, what's that tune?
'All the Things You Are' he tells me.

Tim Liardet
from North Of Everything

for the Chinese cocklepickers drowned in February 2004

The throat at such a distance from the snarling man [...]
    – William Golding, *Pincher Martin*

1.

They go down again, imagine them, spun
in a roaring vortex of gravel, spun

and somersaulted by the force of water,
burning water, bursting in the mouth like gases

or a storm of stones. The throat flung clear
and detached in the depths from each snarling man

is the throat that gulps. They are bound to each other,
all twenty-one, by whatever part of the body

touches at any given second, like a system of branches
struggling in and out – trying to climb –

what might be thought of as a trunk of light.
And they are bucked and thrown about, gulping

at water like buckled tin. They shed coins,
a Wellington boot, their eyes shrink back

into their heads, as if their lips are magnified;
until they are overtaken, overtaken

and the last lit up cellphone spins
to the bottom, spelling out: no network coverage.

3.

They come up. And with them surface
the problems of sea-burial, the question

of what is weighted, but won't stay buried... Those blank
mortuary labels to which they'll be tied –

traversed at night by inky footmarks –
will disclose to us their names, inked-in

like the spirit's tattoo, or the greeting sealed
all the way through a stick of Morecambe rock.

They are spread out and tangled like seaweed
or bleached sea-creatures washed up

on sandbanks two miles out, their lips, their lips
and the twirled weed of their breast-points,

the rock-pools in their clavicles
and swept-over hair the last outcrop – last rock-face –

of a strange obedience. In order to rise, they had first
to sink all the way to the bottom, spilling back

their bucketfuls of cockles before they had
a chance to shake off their Wellingtons.

6.

They come up, like unlosable evidence, turned
to greenish bronze, nibbled by crustaceans;

the muscles of the shoulder-girdle strained,
wrenched and swollen, unequal to the job,

bruised and ruptured, aroused as never before
like something trying to break out of the body;

the monster of survival born in that moment.
Air in the shirt's back panel, ballooning, air

in the underpants, lifted up that weight;
their foreheads, their noses grazed by the sea-floor, the sea-rose

of a haemorrhage worn in the left ear,
each head ducked lower than the body to read

the depths, its slow hair moving in the calm...
each hand clutching something where it was torn off

from the world, fracturing the fingernails.
And in the pockets, not only silt and sea-lice

but heavy stones, stones tied to their ankles
they were told would help them to rise.

8.

They come up. And with them surface
the last bits and pieces of a wrecked vessel

that might have gone by the name of *Albion*.
They come up, and as they come up goes down

the corona of old rhetoric. They roll over, as if
the tides are trying to cover them. Find for us

the culpable, deep inland, say their mouths full of darkness.
Hack off the gangmaster's head, say their hands,

and another one grows. If one gang opens up
another opens up behind it, another behind that...

the words on the warning-boards were not yet
translated into Mandarin, say their stony eyes,

we lived in hovels, paid a pittance, and now our tongues
are frozen in a sort of labial curl.

The tides return, the monster's trapped in the harbour
and now it's all door-bolting rationales

shutting one after the other against the surge:
too soon, too late, too soon, too late.

Steven Matthews
from Essex Coastal

I

Wind-hollows in coarse grass across the Naze,
billows skipped about its inlet waves.
All had been altered here by winter:
wrack trailed its wavy line high up the beach,
shingle had been reshaped in promontories
reaching into the sea, sand hills were re-curved.
The grey concrete of the wartime look-out post,
where we gazed out before the storms, had sheered
further beneath the shale, its piss smell
and desolation vanished tracelessly.
Spring tides breaking beyond the sea wall
had flooded the saltlands. An iron lake
rippled in a field, high-stepped by a heron,
white dab in dim light always about to lurch free.

III

There is something here that will not bear telling.
As autumn sun died into the deep pools left
by the tide's withdrawing, stepping stones,
precarious in the mud, stood starker.
A foundered houseboat, keel mussel-shrouded,
sighed and groaned from the waters trapped within.
From Mersea Island, tankers loomed ploughing
a horizon in the sky through earth's
curvature. Those evenings, when sun lowered
over the expanse of wave-rippled beaches,
opened onto voids of beauty and content.
Plovers darted at movements by the sea's edge.
Those stepping stones joined nowhere to nowhere.
There is something here that will not bear telling.

Andrew Motion
Al Mechanics

Summer sprawling a week into September,
And still muggy at first light when I step out
For milk and papers to the corner store.
No sun for dawn, but claggy cloud-rifts
And plane trees hanging their leaves
Heavy and rusted and stiff as tin.

Where the road bends, the Al Mechanics
Have turned up early – not working yet
But swigging tea in a circle of beer crates.
It could be the old days, and this lean-to
A blacksmith's with carriage horses waiting
For new shoes, noses stuffed in feeding-bags.

If I were living then, I'd find the low roof
Furred with soft cinder-stains, the forge's eye
Widening to crimson as breeze lifts through,
Hammer-clinks chasing their bright echoes,
The thick whiff of burned hoof, and clippings
The blacksmith's dog wants but dare not take.

But I am living now, so I slacken and call
Good morning, which the men choose to ignore,
Or cannot hear above a radio song dropping
Lost love-notes from its hook in the rafters
Down into the sun which now breaks through
With odd bolts of gold into their conclave.

Beautiful, grave world. Your speed in space
And mine have never matched. I am too slow
Always, or too quick, so my shots at everything
Fall short of where I mean to strike and stick.
Love, kindness, work. Work, kindness, love.
But I keep going, and here is the store open.

David Harsent
after Cavafy

The Art Of Poetry

One hell of a fuck and that's it.
They get out of bed. They get dressed.
They don't speak a word. Then they split,
both of them seeming a touch
shaky, now, as they leave
(not together, of course) and hit
the street. It's easy to guess
from each wide-eyed look as they pass
that enough was just too much to give.

Nothing unusual in this,
but the poet has just caught a whiff
of a song coming on (maybe soon,
maybe not) that will start with the line
One hell of a fuck and that's it...

At The Tobacconist's Window

A small crowd at the neon-lit window
and these two, these among many...
Their eyes, as if meant to, snag softly,
something of sex there already,
then they walk off, although maybe
unsure until one smiles discreetly
and catches a nod – only barely.

They drive, they park up... They are so
careful about how best to go
here and go there, lips and hands going slow
as they fall on each other, but gently.

Afternoon Sun

They are renting out the room, this room
and the room next to it, the room
I know so well, they are renting every room
in the house, a house of rooms
rented to agents, to clerks, to businessmen.

A sofa stood by the door, a Turkish carpet
in front of the sofa; on that shelf,
two yellow vases, yes, then, off to the right,
– or was it? – a wardrobe, its fly-flecked mirror,
then the table, a pen, a half-done poem,
three wicker armchairs, yes,
and beside the window, our bed.

(Somewhere, that old stuff must still be knocking about.)

Beside the window, our bed. Yes.
The afternoon sun
crept over it as we lay there: over us.

At four o'clock on one such afternoon
we parted
for just a week... a week or so... forever.

Greta Stoddart
Instrument

All this wind and rain could so easily go
without saying (and it does, we know it does)

and, as ever, birds – no, swifts! fluid,
workmanlike, fixing rips in the sky.

Here we go again, saying stuff;
coming up against this great easy other.

To what good isn't clear but who's to stop us tonight
as we make our beery diesel public transport way home

thinking up a bird (never mind the name),
a small bursting thing – I have him

in a clearing, the world at his feet,
his chest giving in and out like a pedal.

Allison Funk
Penelope At Home

At first light she imagines crimson,
Threads stained with saffron,
The madder root's orange.

But what use if the wool's not
Between her forefinger and thumb – and,
And, this is it: how can she bear to begin,

Start over each morning,
When it's all she can do to dress?
The food she puts in her mouth,

Tasteless. The least wind
Has subsided, she says to herself
As a sailor might to his ship.

How can *she* move it?
The body that through childhood and since
Had borne her, always headed somewhere,

As if possessed of a power
Outside her. Any more,
To go on, she forces the voices

Down, one after the next
Calling from inside her house.
Loudest of all: her son blaming her

For his father's absence
Until she escapes to her loom
Where armed with her *spatha,*

The one sword she owns,
She tightens the weave
To keep him, everything out.

At noon, she vows to have the last word,
But who knows when she'll finish
Her pattern of doubled hearts,

Each lobe coiled like the sea snail
Prized for its drop of blue purple?

Torchlight

Shows her unravelling,
How at night she tugs, she tears out
The strands of her hair.

Dark and graying they fall
As slowly as motes to the floor,
Where the threads she wove by day,

Now unstrung, also lie –
One over, one under the other.
Undone!

The chorus of a hundred mollusks
Sacrificed for their tint
Cry out from the fringes,

Undone.
A shroud, she'd lied,
When asked at first,

Not guessing it would come to this:
Every day she rises
To weave herself one.

Mohammad Hoghughi
All With Wings

I jump from morning sleep,
from the village sleep.
(I jumped
from the cock's crow.)
Moonshine takes off; escapes.

The flock of the sky birds
take to their wings.
I take to my wings,
from rapture.
The distant cloud takes to its wings,
from light.

Under my skin, I sense –
together with the earth's scent –
the flow of the sunrise.
Sleep flies,
and I
become wings.
On the mountain, the distant mountain,
the thousand-winged cock*
takes under its wings
the mass of the sky birds.

In the daylight winds,
frightened, I pull in my wings.
From beyond the town,
my shadow on the ground
can be seen.

"Which way?"
I become the question mark –
past the evening hills.
"Which way?"
The thousand-winged cock
keeps
going
down.

Under my skin, I sense –
together with the town's scent –
the flow of the sunset.
Sleep comes.
Wings fly away.

*Mythological sun.

Translated by Parviz Omidvar and Iraj Omidvar

Nazand Begikhani
Calm

Let's lie down
close our eyes
and listen to the music of the sun
to the grass singing
Let words have a rest
and speech a little siesta

Fred Voss
Starting The Avalanche

I am writing a poem about Joaquin
as he stares at the tin can full of black Molylube
I am swabbing a ¼-20 tap with
he is at the machine next to me
singing
some love song from El Salvador
as chips of aluminum fall
like rolled-up silver petals
from the cutter plowing through the slab of aluminum clamped to the
        table of his machine
he strides
sweating in black tank top before his machine smiling
at me knowing nothing
of this poem I am writing
in my head
For so many years I have been standing next to men at machines writing
        poems about them
will there ever be a day when poems
like this one are tacked up next to the charts of drill sizes
on bulletin boards in machine shops
like this?
When men like me don't have to hide their poems
from the boss
who thinks wearing a white shirt in an office puts him
on a higher plane
will someone like Joaquin
or Carl in the corner on his turret lathe ever want to shout out
these lines?
Shakespeare
Bukowski in toolboxes of men like me who could have been managers
or company presidents
but would rather look for the beauty in a line of words

with machine grease
on their fingers?
Joaquin
rode the top of a boxcar into this country
he knows what it is like to be on a cross like the one hanging
on his chest
Tomorrow I will hand him this poem
and hope it is the pebble that starts
the avalanche.

Peter McDonald
Against The Fear Of Death

As the car boils
with sunshine, stuck,

and my hand feels
around the slippery

pudge and stubble
of my own chin,

in the heat again
that sweetsour smell,

your forehead chill
to the touch with sweat,

our two heads then,
our two faces

(ages past, the same
as now, or just then),

mine against
your frightened face

like the white pages
at the end of a book,

between gasps of pain
as we just waited,

and out there, behind
the slatted blind

that put light in threads
across your eyes,

a bright-blotted sky
too white to look at.

Mustafa Stitou
Coffin

On my back I carried my father's coffin. It was a heavy burden.
With each bent step I staggered until I could not take its weight.
I lay on the ground, slid from under and lifted the cover,
whispered, Father, I cannot carry you. Can you walk with me a little?

After a while his eyes opened. He sighed and shook his head
with that mocking compassion, drew himself up and stepped from the
coffin.
He wore white pants and a white shirt; he was unshaven, his hair tousled.
We walked silently, I behind him; the coffin we left on the path.

We arrived at the grave. It had been dug before us. He lay down
without a word on one side then the other, looking for east, looking for
Mecca,
as his god obliged him. He did not ask me which way to turn,
and I was glad, for I did not know.

He folded one hand on the other to make a pillow and, sighing deeply,
closed his eyes.
I, I fell on my knees and closed the grave, my wild arms waving.

Translated by Sarah Corbett

This October, Mustafa Stitou and Sarah Corbett will be appearing at Ilkley Literature
Festival, Beverley Literature Festival and Poetry International as part of By Heart /Uit Het
Hoofd, an Anglo/Dutch exchange project.

Pascale Petit
Atlas Moth

This giant atlas moth's broad wings
could be the map of China.

Here are two Great Walls. And there
on the Manchurian tip of each forewing

are dragon heads to scare off predators.
But what are those windows in the map

where crystal scales let in the light?
As if earth's skin has windows

and at certain times of the evening
they open. The newly emerged atlas

perches on my hand, and it trembles –
like a new world, warming up for its first flight.

A. A. Marcoff
The Hymn Of The Radiant

it is space & its radial impulses
it is intelligent Eden – the integration of the star
it is the tracts of the mind's time
it is the burnt rust of orange bursting into autumn
it is the hymn of the world

as beautiful as the cadences of tears
as beautiful as reeds – still by green water
as beautiful as the endless mirror
            that is endless with God
as beautiful as cobalt
            (& simplicity itself)
we are caught up
            with pure living
in the sacraments
            of the worlds
we inhere

as beautiful as a petal –
                    pink with a fragile light
as beautiful as anything that is
                    (as clear as morning)
                    (& elemental)
we are as pale fugues –
                    or memories & the lovely music
of our acts
we are
            the distillation of the lucid
            the passage of infinities into passion
& we flow
            from the ground
like sunrise & intent

it is the movement towards colour & water
the dynamics of meaning
the drawing of dream
it is the way we move across the estuary with joy
it is the way we see into the hollow of the bay
& into the rhythm of willow

it is the lily
          of the mind implicit
it is the rite –
          ancient with silences & white
it is in the lilting of the waters of the wave
& in the wine
          shed in the metaphysics of our being here
it is the flower
          offered
          to you
          now
& the future of the spring

it is beautiful like surprise
               like solace
          like rain
          like stone in the sun
it is like light in the green of the forest stream
the inner stillness of an inner sea
the structure of silence & sound
it is the hope for tomorrow – Maria
the hope for sunrise as memory
it is the breath of our being here
or the raw dawn of the diamond

it is the curve of the bird
as though angels were snow
falling through space with all
          the secret geometry
          of snow
          falling
          into silence

it is the pale intelligence
                of mood
the icon of your own mysterious beauty
the sudden elusive impact
            of joy
            in the Absolute

this is the core of the world
the canticle of this consuming blue
it is the chorale
            & the oration
            of the air

because it is beautiful like the names of the rivers
because it is the knowledge of water
because it is the hymn of the radiant
because it is the vacancy of dawn
because it is becoming
because it is because of this
because it is lucid
because it is this
because it is alive with space & voice & flower
because it is now
            this scarlet rose of starlight
            this presence
            this iconic & implicit space –
because we know
            that this is sunrise
            that this is the choral air
            radiant
            as the morning

Jane Holland
Books At Auction

I

I used to arrive early, to wander through the clutter:
tables, chairs, a walnut desk
from the nineteenth century, lampstands
and dolls' houses, the usual array of paintings
by artists no one has ever heard of,
bric-a-brac, porcelain dolls with real hair,
a rocking-horse. There was always something odd
to see there, hold upside-down, poke around in
or sit on. I remember polystyrene cups,
cheap coffee from the kiosk.
They called me 'love' or 'pet', those men
who humped furniture for a living (in
and out), their stained brown coats
that stank of linseed oil, their cheeky offers
of a cigarette.
                I grew muscles
like weeds that year, hefting boxes to the car,
bending my knees. Books, books,
the musty smell of them, like old perfume,
like history – 'To H.B. from Lily, 1904',
'To Mother from your Beloved Son George' –
their marbled end-papers foxed, spotted
like trout, the maps and diagrams
that folded out – the entire midship of a schooner
once, in immaculate condition –
the tiny wormholes and the worms themselves
(killed off by freezing overnight).

Though those paper-thin silences
before bidding began
were often like the silences
of our first nights together – eyes meeting briefly,
then lips – love

is not like bidding for books at an auction
(except for the tension
and never being quite sure what
you'll end up with
or how much it might cost you).

II

Books can be like love though,
a high dark dream of love, a secret *only you and I
can know this* love.
So I'd bid more steeply than intended,
burnt up with lust
for some T.S. Eliot First,
then slip outside for a cigarette
empty-handed
and smoke there in the rain. Like Barbara in Brest,
epanouie ravie ruisselante...
Yet it was always worth it, at the auction,
buying books in competition. Even
the hours spent on my knees afterwards, bent
over those boxes, sorting out
and cataloguing, pricing up, my hands
book-black by the end of it,
dancing and singing over the covers:

Ha! Ha! Among the Trumpets, Alun Lewis;
Loch Derg from Patrick Kavanagh;
Nil Nil by Don Paterson, faded blue cloth,
signed by the author, good condition;
Milton's *Paradise Lost*, calf-bound and gilt
in three volumes, 1795;
the *Complete Poems of Alice Meynell*
on hand-made paper, limited numbered edition;
an early *Crow*, slightly foxed,
with marginalia; Vita Sackville-West,

her modest *Selected* from the Hogarth Press;
Betjeman's *Summoned by Bells*, green cloth
minus jacket, a First Edition.

III

Why buy them, to preserve them? Better
to let cyber-space have them, let them be words
on screen, seen and unseen, corruptible.
That page will fade, data disappear, no safer there
than between hard covers,
yet never so beautiful nor dangerous, something real
to hand on, like a name or a sword.

Say that under our fingers, our eyes
or here on the tongue, a book of light is rising:
the word that we made to be heard – dignified
godhead, salt-washed,
bound bone and blood in it,
went to the stake for it, then lost or discarded –
has been hidden from fire, riddled
with worms, pressed and spotted
by brown wild flowers,
then written-over by notes scribbled
in margins, recipes
laid down on blank versos and these ghosts
on the flyleaf, the dates and names
of the faithful – when bought, when handed on,
where kept, by whom (though rarely why,
the hidden purposes of readers
blown like dust from gilt-edged spines).

Or rather say, look, this is what we achieved
in our age. This is a book.
Open it to the first page and read.

Conversation:
Fish and Bicycle

Gagan Gill
Fish

No water
only sky
fills this fish's brain.

No water
but a longing to fly
is in this fish's body.

Into the brimming ocean
she is emptying herself
incessantly, over centuries.

She passes by
small fish, big fish.
Lost in thought, this fish
asks herself *oh,*
where did your ocean
go?

The swimming fish
repeats this question
as if it were a prayer-mantra.
The fish does not know
that sky has filled
her brain

that the skull-smashing ritual
has already begun
inside her.

Translated by Jane Duran and Lucy Rosenstein

Susan Wicks
Cycling To See The Fish-Ladder

Do they riffle their translucent fins
between the rungs to inch up?
Or do they effortlessly rise
as if through someone's sleep
to do what people do
with ladders – search and replace
a frost-cracked tile, or shake a tree
into a waiting skirt? Each trunk I pedal past
swells and shrills with cicadas before it fades.

But when, blinded by sweat, I finally arrive
the ladder's shut
by a Red Alert. *Merci
de votre compréhension*. I straddle my bike
and read what power means
to fish and spawning-grounds. I think I understand:
a glitch and the dream floats belly-up,
the waters of the Garonne
log-jammed and stinking. There's only the sky's

unbroken blue, the tree's small pool of shadow,
a woman's leaning bike. Nothing you can pull out
in a shining shaft, no wooden feet
to dent the mud,
no uprights you can steady against death.

Andrew Johnston
The Cyclist

Here she comes, or here he comes –
her enormous head wobbling towards us,
his fat little legs pumping the pedals...

They say her skin is whitening,
that she is losing her downy hair –
every day he grows younger:

soon he will be nothing,
soon there will be white light,
unnatural calm, a terrible thirst,

flowers to crush in her miniature fists,
days when the bike says "hyacinth"
and then the chain comes off.

A long wait. No time to waste. Look –
he is pressing down on the pedals,
stretching the skin of the world.

Judith Kazantzis
The Dose

After a night dose of rain,
a steam noses up to the window,

the mangroves, ferns, sea grapes,
like a faint skunk whiff

– distinct from the damp earth after rain,
the rain I was born to, how it

sprang down to my greeting or I would run
with it on my eyelids, drop by drop

during each cloud's downpour;
then we would say, O rain, get to Spain

or those southern parts that really need it –
But here... is this smell

stealing along my path
like a sickbed stranger out of the stinking woods.

Kelly Grovier
Rain, Steam, And Speed

Attention was then squarely
focused on the train –

how its engine emerged from fire
coagulating around the

curve. Then my focus
shifted – I

        grew tall enough
to find the hare in front –
              the machine
retreating to mirage

behind it. Now my mind

returns to the hazy
margins
left
of the track.
        Were those angels
scumbling in the water? Was that

water? My eyes
          seem less and less
instrumental than they were –
              my mind,
like a canvas
        tilting – the air

clumped with oil, still waiting
to be squeezed.

Michael Schmidt
Pangur Bàn

i.

Jerome has his enormous dozy lion.
Myself, I have a cat, my Pangur Bàn.

What did Jerome feed up his lion with?
Always he's fat and fleecy, always sleeping

As if after a meal. Perhaps a Christian?
Perhaps a lamb, or a fish, or a loaf of bread.

His lion's always smiling, chin on paw,
What looks like purring rippling his face

And there on Jerome's escritoire by the quill and ink pot
The long black thorn he drew from the lion's paw.

Look, Pangur, at the picture of the lion –
Not a mouser like you, not lean, not ever

Chasing a quill as it flutters over parchment
Leaving its trail that is the word of God.

Pangur, you are so trim beside the lion.
– Unlike Jerome in the mouth of his desert cave

Wrapped in a wardrobe of robes despite the heat,
I in this Irish winter, Pangur Bàn,

Am cold, without so much as your pillow case
Of fur, white, with ginger tips on ears and tail.

ii.

My name is neither here nor there, I am employed
By Colum Cille who will be a saint

Because of me and how I have set down
The word of God. He pays. He goes to heaven.

I stay on earth, in this cell with the high empty window,
The long light in summer, the winter stars.

I work with my quill and colours, bent and blinder
Each season, colder, but the pages fill.

Just when I started work the cat arrived
Sleek and sharp at my elbow, out of nowhere;

I dipped my pen. He settled in with me.
He listened and replied. He kept my counsel.

iii.

Here in the margin, Pangur, I inscribe you.
Almost Amen. Prowl out of now and go down

Into time's garden, wary with your tip-toe hearing.
You'll live well enough on mice and shrews till you find

The next scriptorium, a bowl of milk. Some scribe
Will recognise you, Pangur Bàn, and feed you;

You'll find your way to him as you did to me
From nowhere (but you sniffed out your Jerome).

Stay by him, too, until his Gospel's done.
(I linger over John, the closing verses,

You're restless, won't be touched. I'm old. The solstice.)
Amen, dear Pangur Bàn. Amen. Be sly.

CENTREFOLD

❧

The note of banishment filled my thoughts with the
enchanted music of mourning.
—Hélène Cixous

Mind The Gap:
On Reading American Poetry

JOHN BURNSIDE

Yet words are not the end of thought, they are where it begins.
– Jane Hirshfield

Not so long ago, a highly-esteemed British poet, someone I hugely admire, described, to a company of which I was part, how he couldn't read a poem by Jorie Graham without laughing out loud. What he wanted to say, he went on, was that her *oeuvre*, with the possible exception of a handful of earlier works, was risible, all smoke and mirrors, a pointless and self-indulgent exercise in experimental twaddle. To say I was taken aback is an understatement and, as a devoted reader of Graham's work, I took issue with this, looking to the rest of the company for support; the rest of the company was, however, peculiarly British and, though each was in his or her own way professionally engaged with poetry, all more or less casually agreed with the sentiments expressed. From there, the conversation moved on to the work of other American poets – by American, here, I mean: originating in the United States – and a consensus was soon reached that America was in a bad way, poetically speaking. The American poem was thin, overly-expansive, self-regarding, pseudo-intellectual and – most grievous of sins – sentimental (the mind boggles, trying to conceive of a sentimental poem by Jorie Graham, but then the work of this astonishingly rigorous artist probably fell into the pseudo-intellectual category). It was also far too bloody long. As a devoted reader of American poetry, and as one who values the contemporary American scene very highly indeed, I cast around for names to counter the general mood of dismissiveness. Charles Wright? A polite, but cool response. John Ashbery? Oh, God, no; he's worse than Graham, though at least he's funny on occasion. Robert Wrigley? Rodney Jones? Linda Gregerson? Eric Pankey? Jennifer Atkinson? Like so many other fine American poets, not really known here. And Brigit Pegeen Kelly? The table was silent. There was, at this point, very little I could say other than to offer that standard, utterly pointless, and – no matter how smug it may sound – far from satisfying riposte.

"You don't know what you're missing," I said – but I didn't feel at all smug, or even 'right' in any meaningful sense. I believe that I am not especially naïve about the gap between British and American sensibilities; and I have studied hard to acquire a necessarily subtle – and detached – appreciation of the traditions and social conditions that helped create that gap, yet I am bound to say that, as the conversation progressed, I felt an oddly personal sense of desolation in realising that these lovers of poetry, who would have taken immense pains to get to grips with contemporary writing from Venezuela, or the Ukraine, could so easily dismiss the one contemporary poetry that, for me, has always been vitally important, and from which I feel I have learned so much; not only about writing and reading, but also about thinking, and about being in the world.

*

Begin by imagining the opening of a poem: a woman is walking her child to the school bus-stop, possibly somewhere in the Midwest. On the way, they see a dead deer, a doe, lying stiff and cold in the grass. This deer is related, spiritually and lyrically, to many others, living and dead – one could fill a decent-sized anthology with American deer poems – but it is also a singular variation on the traditional theme. In this poem, the deer is dead, but it is still strangely unapproachable, still set off at a distance. One thinks of the driver in the William Stafford poem, 'Traveling Through the Dark', who, finding a dead doe on the road, sees "a heap, a recent killing", and, because "it is usually best to roll them into the canyon", drags her off:

> she was large in the belly.
>
> My fingers touching her side brought me the reason –
> her side was warm; her fawn lay there waiting,
> alive, still, never to be born.

The driver is troubled by his predicament: the fawn is still alive, but the dead deer presents a danger to other drivers and, though he hesitates, his final allegiance is to his own species. So it is that, in closing, he tells us:

> I thought hard for us all – my only swerving –
> then pushed her over the edge into the river.

Here, in spite of the speaker's compassion for both deer and fawn, the "heap" he has found on the road is approachable, readily handled, and the vital warmth of the unborn fawn can be felt through the side of the dead mother. Elsewhere, in a poem of Robert Frost's, 'Two Look at Two', the encounter is with live animals, and though a wall separates the two humans from the two deer, there is nevertheless a closeness, almost an intimacy in the meeting:

> A doe from round a spruce stood looking at them
> Across the wall, as near the wall as they.
> She saw them in their field, they her in hers
> […]
> they saw no fear there.

After a moment, the doe is joined by a buck, who seems to interrogate the human couple, daring them to speak, or to "stretch a proffered hand" – and, when the encounter is over, the poem ends with a quiet affirmation:

> Still they stood,
> A great wave from it going over them,
> As if the earth in one unlooked-for favor
> Had made them certain earth returned their love.

One could point to many other 'deer encounter' poems in the American pastoral tradition, but few add so much to that tradition, and work in such organised opposition to the easy conclusions it sometimes calls forth, as the poem I asked you to imagine above, Brigit Pegeen Kelly's 'Dead Doe'. Here, the woman and her child, waiting at the school bus stop, find the dead animal, but they do not – cannot – approach her, as Stafford's driver, or Frost's couple, so easily do:

> The doe lay dead on her back in a field of asters: no.
>
> The doe lay dead on her back beside the school bus stop: yes.
>
> Where we waited.
> Her belly white as a cut pear. Where we waited: no: off
>
> from where we waited: yes
>
> at a distance: making a distance
> we kept.

To begin with, in fact, they cannot even approach her imaginatively: the speaker struggles to describe the scene, constantly tempted by, and refusing, familiar scenarios. Indeed, this opening passage sets the scene for all that is to come: throughout, Kelly refuses the easy appeal of traditional pastoral, or the clear moral predicament Stafford evokes; when she is tempted into images like that "cut pear", she draws back, and insists upon the unbridgeable distance between the dead animal and the human family group. What sets that distance between them is not distaste for a dead, perhaps decaying corpse – or even squeamishness about death itself – and the desire to avoid forced explanations of mortality, but the fear of witnessing some kind of resurrection:

> As we kept her dead run in sight, that we might see if she chose
> to go skyward:
> that we might run, too, turn tail
> if she came near
> and troubled our fear with presence: with ghostly blossoming [...]

From this point onwards, the poem embarks upon a method which Kelly has made her own, a bringing forth of the process of working through a spiritual problem, a kind of extended meditation that is also a thought experiment, aimed at a more or less provisional – one might even say 'fuzzy' – conclusion, reminiscent of dialectic, or that Taoist logical equivalent, where dualism is constantly eliminated by the yin-yang cycle. Of course, the mind rarely settles for the provisional: several attempts are made to fix the image, to say something definitive about what the woman and her child see at the bus-stop –

> The doe lay dead: she lent
> her deadness to the morning, that the morning might have weight,
>   that
> our waiting might matter: be upheld by significance: by light
> on the rhododendron, by the ribbons the sucked mint loosed on the
>   air

– but each is quickly balanced by an antithesis, an open-ended concern for the living, both the deer and the child waiting at the bus-stop, who cannot be protected, cannot be kept eternally safe "in mild unceasing rain", and our final view of the deer sets up a whole new set of possibilities: lying dead, at a distance, "her legs up and frozen", she comes to look like two swans, fighting, or coupling, or "stabbing the ground for some prize / worth nothing, but fought over, so worth *that*".

Now, in an instant, in what Dickinson calls "a certain slant of light", the feared resurrection, the "ghostly blossoming" has come to pass, but in a different, unanticipated form:

> And this is the soul: like it or not. Yes: the soul comes down: yes:
> comes
> into the deer: yes: who dies: yes: and in her death twins herself into
> swans:
> fools us with mist and accident into believing her newfound finery
> [...]

and though this vision is not as frightening as the anticipated "blossoming", the speaker remarks that it should be: a different fear, perhaps, like the fear we owe beauty, or the divine, a kind of sublime panic, as:

> we watch her soul fly on: paired
> as the soul always is: with itself:
> with others.
> Two swans...
>
> Child. We are done for
> in the most remarkable ways.

All the while, language has struggled to make sense of the scene; now we close with a soft, heartbreaking word-play, a beautiful ambiguity. Yet the poem has created in its reader an odd breathlessness, a giddy onrush similar to the rush of a panic attack, not in the usual sense, but in the old, true sense of a meeting with the cloven-footed god.

*

Panic. If ever there was a term that needed redefinition – or rather, clarification – it is this. Panic: "a sudden and excessive feeling of alarm or fear, usually affecting a body of persons, and leading to extravagant or injudicious efforts to secure safety". So *The Shorter Oxford* tells us, explaining that, originally, this emotion was occasioned by an encounter with Pan, whose "appearance or unseen presence caused terror and to whom woodland noises were attributed". Yet this is much less than half the story, and it presents the Ancient Greeks in a remarkably patronising light, as mere superstitious pagans, fearful of the wind in the trees or some looming, possibly spectral predator in the undergrowth. It is a definition that forgets the story of Pheidipides, the Athenian youth who meets Pan in the woods as he is running to seek help from the Spartans against an invading Persian army: true, this meeting strikes terror into the young athlete's heart, but it also inspires him to continue, and gives him the strength not only to finish the round trip to Sparta (where his request for help is denied) but to go on to Marathon and take part in a great victory before running back to the waiting Athenians with news of their salvation. Here, in its Greek original, panic is more than fear, more than terror: it is a glimpse into the fabric of the world, a glimpse, after all, of the divine, and it fills its recipient with an inspired awe, a more-than-human vitality, as well as a terror that, while understandable, is recognisably a by-product of the encounter with the goat-god, rather than the main event.

I would not wish to suggest that this panic has national borders, however. American poets are discovering it anew, just as European poets, from Seferis to Celan to Eliot, rediscovered it in the middle of the last century. One of the most beautiful, perfect and economical expressions of that panic appears in Eugenio Montale's 'Ossi di Sepia'; lacking an English translation of the poem, I quote my own rather loose and profoundly inept version of it here, purely by way of illustration:

> Perhaps, on a day like this, the morning air
> like cut-glass, I will turn around to see
> the miracle:
>
> the nothing at my shoulder, utter void
> caught in the sudden twist
> of a drunkard's terror;
>
> perhaps, like the beginning of a film,
> the world will come again: houses and trees
> and nuzzling hills, returning one by one
> for the grand illusion;
>
> though by then it will be too late
> as I hurry on,
> among those who have never looked back,
> with my given secret.

But what causes this panic? Most fear is fear of injury, or of death, but panic will have none of that. Panic is the fear, not of the unknown, but of the unknowable. At the same time, it is the inspiration, the dark joy, that comes of the encounter with what cannot be known: the sense that something orders the world, the sense that "all shall be well and all manner of thing shall be well", even if we can never comprehend that order and even if we, as individuals, are only fuel to its eternal flame. Panic is the moment when we apprehend the divine in the fabric of the everyday, and see that it moves independently of our hopes and fears, carrying us forward a little way, then letting us fall, easily, naturally, as leaves fall from a tree in the autumn. It is a glimpse of the void itself: that regenerative, all-consuming nothingness from which we all emerge, and into which we are all destined to return.

*

When I was a child, there was a brand of golden syrup that came in a green and gold tin illustrated with a picture of a lion, dead and rotting in the dust, a wave of bees digging in beneath the skin and hair, rendering honey from the dark flesh. People believed this once – that honey came from the bodies of dead animals – but nobody believed it when I was a child, so it was, for me, a first brush with metaphor in its most obvious manifestation, a metaphor of change and continuity that meant more, at some private level of spirit, than the public imagery of church. In a recent poem by Robert Wrigley, 'The Other World', this metaphor reappears, as the poem's human protagonist finds an old buck dead in the woods:

> Here, already bearing him away
>   among the last drifts of snow
> and the nightly hard freezes,
>   is a line of tiny ants,
> making its way from the cave
>   of the right eye, over the steep
> occipital ridge, across the moonscape shed-horn
>   medallion and through the valley
> of the ear's cloven shadow
>   to the ground,
> where among the staves
>   of shed needles and the red earthy wine
> they carry him
>   bit by gnawn bit
> into another world.

It is a beautiful poem, from a poet who can say that the song of a meadowlark "sounds to me like reason", but can also speak, in the same collection, of the true, classical panic:

> Now all rodents are emboldened,
> all owls through their talons knowing,
> down the limb-bones and capillary fretwork
> of roots and holes, that every living thing's
> about to bolt,
> even the tiny dumb animal
> of my sleep, having for how many hours now
> cowered under the rock of possible dreams –
> look, there it goes, a whip of a tail
> running for its life [...]

This, for me, is a perfect foil to 'The Other World': where one speaks of the process by which organic reality is visibly renewed, the other tells of the terror and awe that comes of not knowing, of never being able to know, how that renewal works. As an epigraph to the collection from which these poems come (*Lives of the Animals*, Penguin, 2003), Wrigley quotes D.H. Lawrence: "And as the dog with its nostrils tracking out the fragments of the beasts' limbs, and the breath from their feet that they leave in the soft grass, runs upon a path that is pathless to men, so does the soul follow the trail of the dead, across great spaces." A perfectly appropriate epigraph for this book, but also one that reminds me of another of Lawrence's sayings, "There's not a shadow of a doubt about it, the First Cause is just unknowable to us, and we'd be sorry if it wasn't." As human creatures, unable to bear very much reality, we feel wonder, awe and panic when space opens for a moment and, in a meeting with an animal, or a glimpse of "the force that through the green fuse drives the flower", we see into the fabric of the world itself; a vision that both reaffirms the continuity of that world and leaves us doubtful of our own place in it, other than as creatures to be transformed into new lives, new forms, in which nothing of the flesh and the dreams that are so tender to us can survive. This, for me, is the question that lies at the heart of the most interesting contemporary American poetry, a question that one finds elsewhere, in Spanish and Italian writing for example, but which British poetry tends to avoid, wary of its potential pitfalls: what contemporary US poetry has, it seems to me, is a method – a showing forth of the process of reflection, a revelation of a provisional and ever-shifting internal dialectic – that much British poetry refuses to pursue, informed by a bad faith that says it is better to avoid such matters altogether, in order to avoid any risk of sentimentality, or pretension. Better, it seems, to say nothing well than something badly. Better, of course, to say *something well*.

All of this is flawed, of course. We say different things, and sometimes very little is said at all on either side of the gap. Sometimes we say the same things, and sometimes our methods are not entirely dissimilar. There is, however, a trend in US poetry that I have identified in the poets mentioned above, and in others: this trend of bringing forth the internal process of reasoning, where the poem resembles something improvised, sometimes at the expense of the polish we, on this side of the water, so value. Larkin derided John Coltrane's improvisational method as presenting us with nine possibilities, when he could have chosen just one, and in this he may have had a point. He was also, without a doubt, being deliberately unfair. As unfair as the British poet I mentioned at the beginning, when he spoke of Jorie Graham in such a dismissive way. For, while it is true that Graham could present us with an end point – and only the end point – of her process of reflection, it is also true that this is *exactly what she does not want to do*. What she wants, as I see it, is to reveal a way of thinking, a way of seeing, that is new – new, that is, in the manner that Heidegger called for, when he said that our philosophy demanded a new mode of thinking. This new mode of thinking, and so of being, is based on a fuzzier logic, a more provisional set of parameters, a more tentative notion of the self and a stricter internal life than we have heretofore been prepared to accept.

Most of all, this new mode of thinking demands a new mode of seeing what we thought we had seen – and properly described – before. For instance: what we have tended to think of as nothingness, or – for the more Romantically inclined – the *abyss*, is, if we consider Eastern thought, also the origin of all things, what has been referred to, for want of a better term, as the creative void. A shift in thinking comes with Sartre's notion that *le néant hante l'être*, (nothingness haunts being), at first sight one of those fashionably pessimistic 'existentialist' *bon mots* of the Parisian mid-century but, on closer examination, an idea that proves beguilingly ambiguous. We look into nothingness and we see either a personal abyss or a generative source, a cold void or the moment before the Big Bang, the generator of the initial singularity. Yet nothingness – absence or even, in the Japanese ceramic tradition, boredom – has so often been invoked as the point at which human creativity begins. As John Cage remarks:

> Our poetry now is the reali-zation that we possess
> nothing   Anything therefore is a delight

The new mode of thinking embraces both these ideas, and proposes a synthesis, but, for the individual, this synthesis is founded upon a paradox: as we celebrate the creative power of nothingness, we also celebrate our own erasure as persons; as we lament our erasure in the long continuum of creation, we also lament creation itself, which, to continue, must expunge us from the earth in order to bring new bodies into the light of being.

*

One poem by Jorie Graham, the exquisitely beautiful 'Holy Shroud', (from 1991's *Region of Unlikeness*), begins with the imagery of nothingness, in stanzas that invoke "deadwinter", "empty lot", "stubblefields", "desolation and cold", "sour milks and the acids / of tin". Into this bleak landscape come flocks of birds, "every last cardinal for miles", drawn by a particularly free-fruiting thornberry:

> Now they're lifting as a large cloth would
> into a corridor of sun,
> maybe three hundred sets of lungs
> drifting in unison, showering around this single blade
> of sun like so many
> minutes.

The cardinals haunt the "back of the mall", trying to make a home of that desolation,

> threading in and out of the discarded
> photobooth, necklacing it, trying
> to nest in the plexi face-plate
> someone kicked in
> after maybe three thousand faces had leaned
> their images upon it

– trying, and succeeding, to bring it all to life, "with their bodyweights and tiny / leaps" to draw a "storyline, // down over the whole barrenness". At this point, the poem pivots: the "large clot'" of birds, settling into the place where three thousand faces have "leaned their images", suggests the form – "the face which is His / which is not our looking" – that "emerged" from the Turin Shroud on the night of May 23, 1894. *Emerged* is the important term here, for this poem, and the collection from which it comes, is all about emergence, about what we look for, and what is given, about what comes forth from the world and what must be discovered by imagination, by faith, by doubt. When Secondo Pia was working on "his last attempt at a clear print / of the holy shroud", we are told, the darkroom hummed and:

> A face looked out at Pia from
>
> the bottom of the tray,
>   a face no one had ever seen before
> on the shroud, a face
>   that was, he said, unexpected. A face. A thing
> whose stare overrides
>   the looking.

The sight of this unexpected face causes Pia to faint, as the print "floated / to the surface of the surface / where it lives now." Yet when the shroud is put on public display, "covered with stains and lined with / red silk", the effect is far less dramatic:

> When they held it up to us
> we saw nothing, we saw the delay, we saw
>
> the minutes on it, spots here and there

which is exactly what reason would suggest. The shroud is held up, the sun presses against the façade of the basilica, "like an interrogation light", the shroud's ten keepers stare out into the crowd, and it seems that, like the "tiny heads and bodies of saints [...] and the stone arrows in the stone flesh", this is merely another artefact, a religious image created to encourage the faithful. Yet this – the seeming absence of proof, the nothing, the ground of possibility, the point of emergence – is exactly the point; and the crowd, it seems, know what is required of them:

> we tried to see something, little by little we could almost see,
> almost nothing was visible,
>   already something other than the nothing
> was visible in the almost.

– and so it is that, like the cardinals, we make our place in the world by finding the "storyline", by drawing it down "over the whole barrenness", as we collaborate with what is there and with what is not, making our "tiny leaps" part of a world that emerges, minute by minute, from the almost. In this work, the "nothing" is our responsibility: we see in it what we are able to see, and what we see is true.

*

And this, in the current climate, is what makes American poetry dissident. At one time, dissident poetry seemed only to originate in obviously totalitarian countries, places where ugly dictators with funny moustaches and wide uniforms suppressed even the most minor of liberties. We failed to recognise the creeping advance of what Jonathan Franzen has called "cultural totalitarianism", a mentality that has led us to where we are now; especially in the United States, where the apparent consensus is anti-intellectual, fundamentalist, literal-minded, self-righteous and xenophobic to a degree that has not been seen since the 50s. One of the strongest counter-currents to this cultural totalitarianism is American poetry's insistence on the provisional, on the dialectic, on the bringing forth of the thought process, on the metaphorical. Of course, American poetry has always been dissident; what is new about today's poets is that they not only challenge political and social conventions but investigate a new way of thinking about the most basic facts of existence, and by so doing, demand a new way of being in the world, in an era when the only meaningful existence is one that gives up its limited, ego-based concerns, and dedicates itself to what James P. Carse has called "the infinite game".

Aphorisms

DON PATERSON

He was starting a little poetry magazine, and asked me if I had any advice for a budding editor. The only thing I could think of was *open all the mail away from your face.*

ℬ

Email allows me to indulge my new meditative technique: annihilation via impersonation. I answer each letter in my interlocutor's voice, and forty responses later I am no one and everyone.

ℬ

She insisted on absolute honesty, so I told her everything. I never saw her again, but at least I had spared the next guy the same ordeal.

ℬ

It is not the sophistication but the poverty of a people that is revealed by the local flourishes of their speech. The infinite Sami terms for snow (Eskimos, contrary to popular myth, have need of just two), the eighty shades of green a Nepali can summon by name, are really just the songs of thin economies, which *always* demand this kind of local hyponymic explosion – and are beautiful only to the alien eavesdropper. Scots, for example, has sixty-three words for different kinds of coughing and expectoration, being simply our traditional impediment to work. *Kechle, kisty-whistle* and *black hoast* may even sound charming to you; to me they do little more than explain the absence of our erotic literature.

ℬ

I have owed a slight acquaintance, K., an email for six months. This morning I hear that he has died. My single obsequy was to cross him off my to-do list, and feel my burden lighten a little. I even caught myself wondering if there might be something in this that could be worked up into a general strategy.

ℬ

My plan was to involve her in an act of such intimacy as to both repel and enslave her: I had long understood the power of our disgusted complicities. But nothing could enslave her, *nothing* could repel her; and in reaching my own extremes I realised the game had been hers all along, and that I had already lost my mind months before.

ℬ

No sense steps into the same word twice.

ℬ

The bald ape has committed what is probably the universal *defining* error of the doomed intelligence: it has mistaken its dream for its element. Such carelessness soon sees it translated to the wrong one, where it finds itself irredeemably grounded, beached, drowned. If we're typical, no wonder the skies are silent.

ℬ

Her so suddenly quitting in the early stages of our relationship meant I was obliged to hurriedly revise my future; at least this afforded me, I decided, the bravery of a blank canvas I might not otherwise have been granted. Unfortunately, the new ventures and career-paths I proposed for myself – street-vendor, lunatic, rapist, drunk – seemed oddly in the grip of certain imaginative constraints.

ℬ

Fate's book; but my italics.

ℬ

Writers can redeem a wasted day in two minutes; alas this knowledge leads them to waste their days like no one else.

ℬ

He liked to think he was a thorn in our side; but he was a much smaller man than he imagined himself, and merely a pain in the arse.

Three Extracts from *Manhattan*

HÉLÈNE CIXOUS

I Loved Above All Literature

I loved above all literature ever since the death of my father my being had a definition of quite extraordinary precision that kept me and it from anything that was not literature, now this is the life I thought at dawn I would crack open a book by Stendhal and "the light" darted out; "the light" is this sudden, colourless switching on, all inner fire which, in principle, takes place whenever I get close to a sheet of paper book or notebook page, providing the condition of solitude is fulfilled. I open a book, the light is, right away the tongue begins its tale, I'm forever remaking myself with these literary molecules I told myself, then as now, it is six o'clock in the morning maybe seven, I hear the regular and strangely powerful breathing of the books on my shelves. Since the death of my father, they've been breathing like human cats. I was writing a thesis on the note-of-banishment-in-Shakespeare. Thirty-five years ago banishment was unable to play its poignant music except in Shakespeare. I did whatever I liked. I lived where I wanted to. In Stratford, in London, in Illyria, elsewhere. The note of banishment filled my thoughts with the enchanted music of mourning. Who cared about the rest of the world? I had reading for all time. I had left Paris and its Schools, where they didn't want you says my mother because you were a young divorcee, a pity, says my mother, not at all I say luckily they wouldn't have me in the Schools, luckily even before I got in I was banished but right away, in return, I banished Paris, the Schools, in Paris I'd have had to bend my thinking and it would have leapt right back up and smashed everything. Right after my son George's disappearance I took to the roads of literature I kept my distance from cities and schools, and I left to study the theme of banishment, whose music had a familiar ring, in manuscripts conserved in the USA thus safely banished by a process of paradoxical safe-keeping. Passionately and reverently, off I went to consult the manuscripts, the radiant remains of the to-my-eyes-holy works, which the Europe of Schools would have none of whereas the voracious American Libraries had clearly longed for these relics fortunately collected and kept on the far shores of banishment where, later on, from the places that had seen the birth of these grains of light you crossed countries and oceans to go and share the miraculous bitterness of the experience of pascality that never ceases to repeat itself, again and again throughout time. I also went to consult the manuscripts of *Ulysses* and of *Finnegans Wake* in their mad diaspora, with tears in my eyes, I was indignant even as I rejoiced at the blind behaviour that brings the political organism and the individual organism together. Either the body (political, individual, cultural) is good-natured about its most precious organs, its poets, its artists, its eyes, its dreams, or it is not and it begins to bomb and chase away its kings, its queens, its prophets, till they are fed up, never is it the least bit grateful for the apples of its own eyes.

Feverishly I went after banishment, why did I die of boredom in schools I ask my brother when I arrived here from Africa, on the run, finally I'd escaped Algeria which didn't want me till I no longer wanted Algeria either. I am observing our childhood from the balcony of this house says my brother and I see that you have never ceased chasing after the trace of banishment, look at this house, I would die of boredom here, you have shut yourself up in the outskirts of a city god-awful to behold in which you never set foot, I see that in the end you have banished yourself to a building that's a lot like a paperback book. – If I'd left Algeria and our childhood of regret and powerlessness it wasn't so I could end up in France, I took the boat as soon as I could in my life so as to put some distance between me and one shore (and not to get to the other shore the very idea of reaching the other shore horrifies me, I never wanted the other shore except lost in advance, except vanishing, as disquieting and fascinating as it was desirable and repellent just like the dream shores of Lake Averno in which the unreal landscape with its veil of sulfurous fumes is merely the hint of imaginary countries) once and for all I took a ticket for getting away from, not for getting close to and at this I was a great success, the getting away I got it and I never again lost it on a boat I had no port of arrival in view even when I took the giant boat for the USA it certainly wasn't for the USA but for the Library thus secretly for my home base at no permanent address where those whose gift is for banishment are wholly embraced and taken in, the idea of banishment being respected there without being capitalized on, there is no professional banishment, nor is there any enrichment, only a tent roof over the camp site. In the USA I didn't go from city to city but from one Library to the next, and even from one manuscript collection to the next. In my mind I took the boat that was anchored between the columns of the British Museum for the monumental Beinecke Library, even if in reality I had to cross cities roads ports oceans ports cities airports roads that went from Paris to London to New York to New Haven to Buffalo. I wasn't about to be separated from the theme of my complicated but meticulously organized trip: I went straight for literature as banishment. I wanted to interview the giants. All I wanted was to spend my life with the giants, no one else only the giants with giant works. I didn't know myself at all and I didn't interest me. I simply loved Literature as Higher Monstrosity. I enthused over corpses changed into pearls *Full fathom five thy father lies, those are pearls that were his eyes* over and over I repeated the magic words and nothing bad could happen. Literature changed the corpse of my father that was all I asked: the sublimation of the corpse, I tell my brother, is what I was looking for.

I got over the terrible suffering of the cemetery, that we shared, with a book I say to my brother. I never went back to the cemetery. I would read. I went right past the body on into sentences. I made a sentence of my father. I wasn't losing papa any more I say. I wasn't losing any more. I had found the pearl mine. Whoever finds pearls finds pigs as well said my mother, but the pigs I put down to her taste for proverbs. I was possessed: I didn't know it. It never crossed my mind I was losing in another way: I was on the brink of perdition. I didn't see that I didn't see myself. I was losing losing and so high up on the shelves of clouds that I had no alarm system, conscience, presentiment. I was adrift in change. I would read. Everything that could be done with a book in hand I did. Scarcely had I given birth, quick, Montaigne, I would laugh to see the new face of my son, the other one the one after, I no longer thought about the one before, I went on, no turning back, on and on I read and no nostalgia no sooner born than he too is a future reader of my Montaigne who had already read and sketched his newborn portrait foresaying everything the speech of the hands as of the head, and the eyebrows and the shoulders there is no movement that doesn't speak Montaigne I told my newborn son. And there is no creature I read to my infant whom Nature has not provided with everything he needs to survive: shells husks bark hair wool leather under-fur feathers scales fleece silk claws teeth horns weapons clothing and just as the elephant grinds and sharpens the teeth it uses in war (having some special ones it keeps for this purpose and never puts to any other use), so to strengthen its mind and body the child has his stock of books. There are books for war and books for peace, books to complain with, others to rejoice, books to call to one another for help, books that bid us to love. Whatever I couldn't do with a book I did fast, without leaving the beloved in my thoughts, and as soon as the child was bathed and dressed, I would go back to my book I laughed at its wit. I couldn't not laugh. For me literature has always been the greatest and most sublime of affairs the only one that makes me laugh in the midst of the torment.

ℬ

More And More Notebooks

More and more notebooks, I am now writing on a dozen notebooks whose dis/superposition on my desk, due to my convulsive movements, now coming alongside, now nervously pushing off again – (but I don't throw out, I push off) depicts my state of panic – I write in skirmishes. Big notebooks, as against my normal fidelity to small notebooks. In fits and starts followed by brusque abandons. A big broad brand new white notebook seems to call up the spirit of initiative. But in the end I get lost among these wounded, rejected tablets. At which point I go in search of myself. Recall a page of notes that seems to me to have been, to still be I hope, the one that might survive the hecatomb. I can't find it in the ruins, I dig, one writing day lost scrabbling in upside-down convulsions of convulsions that have dispersed the sheet of paper that I hear, I think, breathing – gasping under the landslide. I scratch, I think I find, all these sheets look alike, all these pale blue notebooks, not-to-find to this point what does that mean I thought, the harder I search the more I lose, it seems I am burying what I am trying to exhume, "nobody can see me" I tell myself (every now and then I switch pens as if I absolutely couldn't do without the help of a stronger or more tenacious pen, furthermore I ought to scratch out all the as if's because there aren't any, in this state of mind there is no distance, it is painful, an aching right to the bone, mental, but to the bone, to the nerve) but "nobody can see me" my thought thinks, this is not a complaint or a consolation it's a relief, here I can let myself go in a frenzy of self-bewitchment, a ferocity of intention well-known to the great virtual-criminals, this is furthermore how you know born-scribblers for whom nothing can put a halt to the crisis of writering (I don't mean writing, this takes place beforehand in the understory of the writing, before the appeasement) no intervention or ethical or police influence, no emergency can pretend to be more urgent than the frenetic mental nervous urgency of coming to terms, finding the term for it, often it's a matter of a word, a phrase, a page, an illumination, a nugget, buried, promised palpitating that still gasps in the caved-in shaft but risks going to ground from one moment to the next in the old days the cry of a child might have torn me from the mine and off I went into the next room, thirty years ago, I extracted myself, I was extracted from the vital wallowing, but in what kind of a state, my soul scraped inflamed, mind still stuck in the mouth of the den

and thirty years ago, I sped, mindless, forced – to the side of the child, the only obligation to which I deferred, giving in to the fear of a punishment whose self-flagellation would in the end cost me more than the loss of energy caused by the lacerating displacement of my body from one room to the next. Thus, in the old days, I deported myself, to spare myself. Now only a maternal deathbed could disrupt my frenzied sacrament. "No one can see me" and no one has ever seen me in a trance and it is better thus. "No one can see me" I told myself to shore up my total absence of shame, fortunately no one can see me, fortunately the-thought-of-my-mother has gone to the market along with my mother, that's why no obstacle to the necessary sabbath, more powerful than any convention.

You would recognize us (frenzied writers and myself) in the body of the cat whose spine paws tail are so tightly coiled by the mental covetousness awakened in them by the thought of prey that every fraction of a centimeter hums with an electrical charge whose effect is to contain all bounds under the skin, here life and its suspense touch.

This tension which takes the mind with body in tow to the brink of death, we know, how we know I don't know, it eludes the social contract, it crosses the invisible but wall-like line, thick perceptible to your hands to your forehead to your footsteps, which separates what is universal acceptable human from the unacceptable. Perhaps, I told myself, on a day a little less mentally searing, a week ago, when I was wondering at these seethings, it's that there is a kind of death-and-gore effect, involuntary but undeniable, at moments when the Crisis takes over: no place for anyone else around the bewitched, which in fact amounts to a sort of virtual assassination. Annulation reigns. Everything is wiped out, annulation, annular, there's only circle, annulus, ring, secret message.

Hence the crazy multiplication of notebooks: what seems mad is on the contrary the effect of keeping madness at bay, an attempt to loosen the stranglehold. But the means of defense itself is taken hostage by the trance it wants to escape. Only a miracle from the outside will release the creature back to its element. Its efforts to free itself hasten its demise.

What is even more confusing in my search for the sheet of paper that I've convinced myself might be the shibboleth, is the page numbering. All the beginnings are numbered 1,2,3 (never more) occasionally starred, or perhaps ABC, but since each time I start a new notebook I believe that this is the one that is going to take over, I relapse into naïveté, this one, I think, is the real one, the good one, the first one you don't expect me to write "fourth" or "twentieth" beginning. I believe in the beginning. I believe in the beginning among all the beginnings. I believe that among all the beginnings that finally gave birth to the first of my texts, the one that dragged itself still breathing out of the chaos, after which came other things as sticky and primitive as the original survivor, and after that those I finally agreed to call books started to turn up, I believe, but without any certainty, that there is one, that caused, that made a dint in the chaos, an event among all the events, that deeply nicked the soul. Without any certainty.

What I'm thinking of is this dint, this nick. Of this wound among the scratches.

In any case I believe in an Ursache. *It's around here somewhere. It's not a point. It's not a letter. Besides there is no letter-sign-alone, a letter is always surrounded by all the other letters. A letter is not without its swarm of other letters. But in the swarm there is the cause.*

The Cause is – somewhere in a chaos you need a chaos – invisible to the naked eye – that which brings two absolutely contrary forces into contact – like God's finger suddenly landing, among all the millions of possible surfaces or crevices, precisely on the spot chosen by an absolute violence, why this one among the millions; and the finger of God which has no hand is the Devil. God puts his Devil down: there – which is to say: here. The area around is irradiated, the entire zone is a scene pocked with fateful ricochets. What happens: in the entire area around the point of impact (you don't know exactly where or at what time God's Devil landed), hundreds of millions of traces are set down as in a kind of library.

The most ordinary details emit flashes or blinks of some kind, they cease in truth to be details in order to become signs, messages, proofs. And it is this peculiar life of what is lifeless, this sort of speaking, but mysterious but perceptible, which fills even the most modest objects in the part of the world struck by God and his Devil, which shows this neighbourhood or place, city, airport, to be a scene with a cause. An originary scene. Everything in it is infiltrated, grazed, a particle of complicity. Generally the scene is clearly localized. It has an address. In the Bible too. Earth-shattering encounters have an address. In the picture there are animals, mammals, insects, moths, rocks, inhabitants, a fountain or a well. Each element glows and signifies. Nothing is unnecessary nothing is not fateful. Somewhere in the scene, in the sometimes extensible but always localized perimeter, is the germ of Cause, cause among Causes which hits the target, like the one bomb among all the bombs released that hits the bull's-eye.

℘

Sometimes I'm tempted to say: here's the Cause. *Die Ursache.* The cause of all these sighings and sufferings, not to be regretted. Everything that happens is due. The cause of the relapse. Although for there to be a relapse, there needs first to be a lapse. The cause of my aberrations of all sorts and degrees: ever-impassioned and passionate errors of love, errors in judging people in whom I have confidence, taking my chosen path to extremes: once you take the first step, straight on to the end, straight on to the end. But such is the nature of love-in-anguish as Freud so often said, and in vain. You don't see yourself take the first step. The cause of all my books, of each one, then the next, and the one after that, of their engendering, in a word all my blinkered attempts at de-blinkering, at dis-enclaving, at dis-anguishing, all bound to fail which doesn't keep you from trying. One small lens. I could write the book of the lens also, an epic of the dreams of the lens and the tragic therefore comic adventures or vice versa comic therefore tragic caused by these magnifying glasses, prisms, lens, glasses: lost in the corner of my eye or dropped and ground to bits, or shattering suddenly into dozens of flakes, or swallowed by the ocular throat stuck in the esophagus, or reduced to a third of their small surface, thereby making sight halting and equivocal, etc.

But it is a temptation.

With this magnifying glass you can also set fire to your own bed. This happened to Ingeborg Bachmann, the sole explanation for the fire that was the end of her in 1973. "Disappeared tragically in Rome when the bed in her hotel room went up in flames," the jacket copy says. Disappeared. You can disappear because of what surrounds these lenses, women especially. Nobody warns you. Stendhal tumbled off his horse into ridicule again, but he told us. Proust too stumbled into one destiny instead of another, at least as narrator. As far as Albertine was concerned he was sure that it might not have been her he loved, it might have been someone else. (*Supu – c'eût pu –* he writes in his manuscript in the French National Library.) If only Madame de Stermaria hadn't begged off the evening he was to dine with her, her I mean, he thought. But he would have had to read the letter with his glasses on, to see that the handwriting was not Madame de Stermaria's but the other's, Albertine's. Now for Albertine to be pursued so, as she believed, after thinking that she had written an utterly unanswerable letter caused her to waver in her refusal to let the narrator love her. Albertine's refusal would have kept the narrator from letting it be her whom he loved. Glasses are the authors of momentous events and of wars just as much as and more insidiously than the eccentricities of people. But once they had eaten together, Albertine becomes the one, and only death can put a halt to the enchainment.

In love-in-anguish you really feel that (had you known) you could never have loved the being you-love-forever, all along you feel love threatening you, but you don't know it. The more you feel, the more instinctively you ward it off by increasing the love thus the anguish.

I was bewitched. Can you talk about being bewitched by a lens? Yes say I. I was bewitched by this lens. I dreamt of it. Through that lens I saw everything, and I saw it askew. Secretly the lens played tricks on me. I was always afraid I would lose it. Furthermore I *did* lose it. I never found it in its place. I walked on eggshells for it might be anywhere. A demon. And it was the apple of my eye. Like a demon it turned me into someone with double visibility. I could see that people didn't see me exactly. I myself looked askance. Let me be talking to someone, the lens got involved, but secretly, it was forever ordering me around and making threats. What if suddenly it took the stage?

A foreign body you take in like an insidious body and indispensable commander of the most indispensable sense, sight. In those days, in thrall to the lens as to an impotent and perverse master, I thought nothing. Everything was locked up tight. Was it faking, what I did? I believe I acted guilty. Objectively speaking, there's nothing wrong with wearing glasses. But nothing is objective. I was doubly flawed vision-wise; on the one hand I saw nothing; on the other hand to this original sin I added the extra lens that was supposed to wipe out the sin.

The Detail makes the Tragedy. No atrocious Tale possible without the tiny crack in the wall around the unspeakable. Othello is contained in a handkerchief. This Handkerchief turns anyone who touches it into a monster. The Detail is this seepage and this handkerchief, which hides-shows, gives on the scene impossible to behold. The Detail is the representative and representation of the act of mutation that turns people like you and me into the monsters of Tales. The Detail is a visual shibboleth, terrible to behold. Whoever sets eyes on it will never again be the same. Most of the time, when you enter the Tale, you pass over the Detail without noticing it. In the story it gets misplaced among a host of signs. It was only many years later I caught sight of the Detail which lets us in to *The Metamorphosis (die Verwandlung)* though it is perfectly visible in the entry where it vegetates and stinks, the eternal cadaver left as warning to the reader. But as it doesn't call out or moan or squeak the avid visitor whips indifferently by the prophetic vignette and barges into the front room from which he doesn't emerge alive. If only you'd read the warning Nothing wouldn't have happened. But by definition the Detail hides what it shows.

"Representative Writing"…?

In May, Spread the Word and the Arts Council of England published *Free Verse*, a report into the lack of publishing opportunities for Black and Minority Ethnic poets (www.spreadtheword.org.uk/freeverse). The report articulates the contemporary situation so thoroughly that it would be a disservice to paraphrase it here. However, as a partner in the follow-up *Complete Works* initiative, *PR* invited a baker's dozen of stake-holder writers and editors to respond from their own standpoints, whatever those might be, to some of the issues it raises. Our invitation e-mail spoke of wanting to celebrate, in Louis MacNeice's words, "the drunkenness of things being various". Their responses – in poetry, fiction, mini-essay and even a prose-sonnet agony-column – are by turns practical, creative and, finally, celebratory. Reading them alongside extracts from the Algerian French theorist Hélène Cixous's autobiographical novel – in which she explores the necessity of reading, and writing, to her sense of self – it's impossible to avoid asking what made the Paris of the 70s and 80s a place where such brilliantly transgressive – indeed "alien" – thinking could enter and transform "high" culture; and how that differs from twenty-first century UK.

Daljit Nagra
My Father's Dream Of Return

Booming the clouded mountains,
hurtling around and downwards –
the bird-like, plane-like jet
descent of his car speckling
the slant of goats, fast-brake
at the ceremonial elephants,
downwards for the cows mothering
on the plain, fourth gear
he hooters leathery skin
that climbs on husky trees,
some hands fanned into waves
from sunflower fields, some twisted
heads from the sugarcane. Soothing
his engine by the cesspool,
air-conditioned, he awaits
his audience.

My father then imagines
his old village as a ghost
home with its doors padlocked
creaking for the landlord profiting
abroad, yet men are stooped
to the point of his burgundy loafers,
with the old, in the dust, who launch
prayers to ascend their stares
from the gold hooping him.
He raises the boot of his Ambassador –
nectars children with boxes
of chum-chums, or cool
sherbets in plastic pipes,
shares out tubs of powder
paints and gunned rainbow
liquids, and elastic party hats.
My father dreams of scattering
fireworks through the sun
on everyone!

I'm plonked on his overall'd knee
catching at scabs of cement
on his breast pocket after his return
from work, as he pictures his built
frame in pin-stripes, with voice
blaster than the temple speakers
he'd summon them all to my
wedding with an alabastered
family we'd keep company.
He'd tell them we live over there –
on top of the married mountains
sipping mauve faludas, as we size up
queues of customers (side
by side, in the forecourt shade)
to our almighty BP
stop!

℘

Saradha Soobrayen
As I Am

I exist as I am – that is enough.
– Walt Whitman

My borders are porous.
Which colour are you from?

I am rather turquoise, sinking
into self delusion.

And the purpose of my poetry?
Fame and Glory.

How long will I be staying
in the place between the rhetoric

of my skin and this line?
My thoughts enjamb

around a corner, curious thoughts,
so therefore I am. Regardless

of race or sexuality my poems
are resemblances of many selves.

I am listening for my opening lines,
waiting for myself to appear.

I have doubted that the 'I' exists,
'I blame the twilight for coming too soon'.

Ah, the emphatic 'I': praise,
blame, loss, love. Yes, the DNA

of the poem exists in the first line
along with my slippery self,

unknowing, a kind of bliss.

'I blame the twilight for coming too soon', is the first line of Saradha Soobrayen's
poem, 'On the water meadows', in the Third Poetry School Anthology, *I Am Twenty
People!* (Enitharmon 2007).

E. A. Markham
from *At Home With Miss Vanesa*

The novel manuscript was still held at her old university, pending revision. It had been supervised – either supervised or assessed – by someone Pewter knew, but he probably wouldn't admit this to Miss Vanesa.

So the novel existed. This was not the case of someone sitting here on her verandah all the while claiming to have been Queen of England without giving any hint of the date of your accession or the year of your State Funeral. Though, of course, Miss Vanesa was very much alive – and not even an old woman at that. And talk of her being a fraud was unkind in another sense because bits of the novel had been published in a magazine in England and in a couple of places back home. So the evidence was there. But Miss Vanesa wasn't out to persuade: either you accepted that she was a novelist or you didn't. She had never kow-towed to people in England during her long years of residence in that country; nor was she prepared to do that now to the jackasses on the island. (Here you had to live a life of censorship: if you were driving along a country road, in the afternoon after the rain, and you happened to be in a reflective mood at the too-sexual greenness of everything; and you were with a friend, and you expressed your feelings about the greenness of things, and wondered if it wasn't better to live in places where leaves changed colour and fell in the autumn, they would look at you as if this was a woman thing, and you were in need of counselling.) But then the jackasses here were no worse than the Secret Racist Society at the university over there who, when they read her novel, having run out of excuses for failing it, had charged her with an excess of sensibility. In the days when she bothered to discuss these things she would pose the simple question: how does a woman, sensitive to lewd glances and conversations inside the heads of strangers and passers-by, aware of the glances as she went about her business, and the silent conversations she had no difficulty providing a voice-over for – how was she not to be in a heightened state of awareness *as her normal mode*? She was a woman. And colour would be a feature in this: to internalize and acknowledge all that 'consciousness' didn't seem to her as 'excess'.

[...] The names you called people. A lot of people had been reduced to ordinariness by taking on safer names when they left the island. Take Pam*ela*. Pamela would have grown up, grown to womanhood, and made love with someone calling her by that name. Suddenly, she finds herself in England where everyone called her something else, *Pam*ela, as if she were something sanitized and coming out of Jane Austen – or, if you like, Samuel Richardson: surely, after that she would have to make love – she would expect to make love – *differently*.

℘

Patience Agbabi
from Problem Pages

Two Loves I Have

Dear Patience I'm a poet who writes for the stage and thus pigeonholed a performance poet. However, my plays are on the GCSE syllabus so my poetry stands up on the page. I've recently written a long sonnet sequence addressed to a white man and a black woman. My publishers claim it will confuse the reader but I suspect homophobia/racism. Please help!

I empathise. When will people stop categorising and embrace the page-stage, black-white, heterosexual-homosexual continuum? I applaud your achievements! But who is the reader? Seek critical advice and/or ditch the publisher for one who'll take risks. Your solid reputation will help.

The White House

Dear Patience I'm a Jamaican troubadour wanderer who's published two collections in the UK/US. I challenge racism and classism in classical sonnets in Standard English. My recent anthology submission, *The White House* was retitled *White Houses* by a Black editor. It's not white publishing houses we're barred from; it's the edifice of the American dream.

Congratulations for publishing on two continents! The editor was wrong not to consult you, though he/she may have done it to protect you. Publish it elsewhere under the correct title. And, why not shake some foundations writing classical sonnets in patois? A progressive publisher's dream.

Knew White Speech

Dear Patience I'm a Black female Chicagoan poet whose first collection ended with an off-rhyme sonnet series in the voices of African American officers, resurrecting the controversy about Black poets using traditional white forms. I've been accused of degrading the sonnet with Black, anti-war propaganda: and of not being Black enough!

Some say poetry+politics=propoganda. That Blackpoet+sonnet=sellout. I hope your 'propaganda' sells out, continuing the long tradition of both political poetry and Black poets engaging with white forms. It's literary skill that counts: always ask yourself, am I poet enough?

1) 'Two Loves I Have': inspired by 'Two loves I have, of comfort and despair', Sonnet 144, William Shakespeare.
2) 'The White House': inspired by 'The White House', Claude McKay.
3) 'Knew White Speech': inspired by the opening sonnet of the sonnet series, 'Gay Chaps at the Bar', Gwendolyn Brooks.

Parm Kaur
Notes For A Debate On Identity And Representative Publishing

Let us begin where we began – in darkness: a darkness in which there was yet no colour to the skin, no distinction between thine and mine, no tangle of tongues, no falsely alluring ideas, … no mean emotions, treacheries, promises, prohibitions, no life-long let-downs. – William H. Gas*

In the darkness who are we? Identity as a site for literary analysis and critical studies is not a new phenomenon and now, in this post-modern age, is an integral part of many academic disciplines including literature, drama, the visual arts, sociology, psychology, psychoanalysis, politics and, increasingly, social policy.

But in the darkness who are we? Our definitions of ourselves are most commonly in reference or relation to something 'other' than ourselves: e.g. I am a daughter, not a son. I am not a mother. However most of these definitions require the expression of a linguistic formulation. The kind of language we use and how we deploy it has been seen, since Socrates, as an indicator of character and place.

So what are we without language?
Why is this debate on representative publishing important?
Why do I read?
Why did I read so much, as a child, unlike my brother? If it isn't a gene which determines our propensity towards words – what was/is it? A hunger for stories – of other worlds, lives, realities, ideas, a jumping off point for the imagination, an intellectual curiosity…?

It was not until I was an adult that I actually came across a book, a novel, which was as familiar to me as my own story*. The shock of reading it was akin to that of having a bucket of cold water thrown over me. Reading could be something more than entertainment, voyeurism, escapism, fact-finding or knowledge forming: reading could be an affirmation – not only in a psychological, emotional, spiritual or intellectual fashion but also in real terms describe a very similar (childhood) reality to mine.

Oh! I wondered, what would it be like to have this all your life?

This current debate is about more than this of course – are poetry publishers 'representative'? Have they ever been? Should they be? Perhaps not, however shouldn't spending tax payers' money imply a certain sense of responsibility – if not talent, imagination, open mindedness, intellect, wide reading? If the current publicly funded poetry editors are not selling poetry, not publishing widely enough and have their heads stuck in the sand, perhaps it's time for them to go?

* *Exile. Altogether Elsewhere* ed. M. Robinson (Harvest, 1994)
* *Anita And Me*, Meera Syal (Flamingo, 1997)

ℬ

Eva Salzman
Under The Radar

D on't you hate it when the man at the Islamic literature table in Wood Green bellows into his loudspeaker how he's going to come and get your "women and children"?
Don't worry. He only means us Jews.
Aren't you appalled that Jews are officially barred from certain countries? Don't you hate it when this happens to you?
Or doesn't it?
Anti-semitism is, after all, a minority issue, which is precisely the point. To paraphrase Jewish ritual, this brand of racism is somehow different from other racism... because of Israel. Debate on anti-semitism almost invariably becomes debate about Israel's right to exist.
A tolerant society must tolerate intolerance, including tolerating those who cynically exploit this fact, with under-the-radar anti-semitism. But when such worrying attitudes become mainstream, seeping unnoticed into cultural commentary and eminent literary journals – among the liberal left especially – it's a whole other ballgame.
In March, *London Magazine* published Anis Shivani's "literary criticism" which targeted women poets who write from, and about, their Jewish heritage. The nerve of those broads!
Is it conceivable that any other religious/ethnic group would be criticised for doing likewise?
Responses to the article were telling*. Some declined to comment on the anti-semitism publicly – if they noticed it – for fear of being tagged anti-

Islamic. Others advised that tackling the anti-semitism rather than the misogyny (*whatta piece*, eh?) was self-defeating. In this way self-censoring aids bigoted thought. It seems that the tacit acceptance of anti-semitism is a price worth paying in the battle against... racism.

Few distinguish "Zionist" from "Jewish". It's naïve not to notice who you're standing with, under the anti-Zionist umbrella. Many seem unaware how many Israelis are opposed to the actions of their own government, which no more represents all Israelis than Blair and Bush speak for all their constituents. (If facts stand in the way of prejudice, well then form your opinion without them.)

Anti-semitism is the invisible, tolerable racism. Perhaps a scapegoat is essential to our social equation?

Tick one box for Race and Religion. For secular, cultural Jews like me – for the kind of writer I aspire to be – there's no box to tick; unless you put me into one. If there's an "Other" box, I sometimes tick that. Or you could stuff us all into the same box, and send us back to where we belong. Wherever that is.

* For Eva Salzman's own response, see *London Magazine* June/July 2006.

ℬ

Satish Kumar
Representing The Landscape

From the ecological point of view the landscape is not what we see out there and describe or 'represent' in words or pictures. The outer landscape is part of an inner landscape.

The idea of 'representing' a landscape in words, pictures or through pressure groups, indicates a separation between the observer and the observed, a dualism between the subject and the object.

Ecology is rooted in the idea of 'only connect'. We do not represent the landscape, we experience it as a living system of which we the observers, painters or poets are an integral part. Being in the landscape is a holistic experience.

In Chinese landscape paintings we rarely see trees, hills and rivers alone. There is usually a small human figure or figures in the panoramic view of nature. Humans are as much part of the landscape as the dancing trees, flowing streams, and rolling hills.

From the Indian point of view, the making of art or poetry or the cultivation of soil is a form of meditation, a practice of Yoga. Art and poetry are not a matter of self-expression but a way of self-realisation, which happens when we are able to identify ourselves completely with the living earth and with the unity of life.

A tree can be as much a poem as a verse written on a piece of paper. A hill can be as much a painting as a picture is on a canvas. In ecological art and poetry self perceives self; there is no separation, no notion of exploring nature to satisfy the ego. There is an absolute unity between the artist, the art and the imagination. Ecological art is not merely illustrative, or descriptive; it is a celebration. It is experiential, imaginative, metaphorical, mystical, magical and reverential, full of awe and wonder. It is spiritual and sensual, challenging and soothing, nourishing and inspiring. It is to look at a part and see the whole, as in the poetry of Blake:

> Hold infinity in the palm of your hand
> And eternity in an hour.

It is an ode of devotion, like the songs of Rabindranath Tagore:

> My passion shall burn as the flame of salvation
> The flower of my love shall become the ripe fruit of devotion.

From the ecological and spiritual perspective poetry is not only the lines on a piece of paper; it is life itself, poetry reflecting in life, life reflecting in poetry. One ancient Indian text, Shilpa Shastra, says that:

> The poet is a good human being, generous in spirit, not given
> to anger, holy, learned, self-controlled, devout, charitable and
> taking delight in the care of the self and the care of the earth.

Here there is no distinction between art and the artist, poet and the poetry. Art is not just what we do but who we are. The art emerging through such an artist is not about the landscape, it is of the landscape.

Once I visited an Aboriginal community in Australia. I asked people there, "What do you do for a living?"

"We are all artists", they answered. I was amazed to hear that reply. For them art was neither a representation nor a profession, it was a way of life. They collectively worked on the canvas, men and women of all ages contributed to a painting, even children joined in. For them art, living, landscape, mythology and poetry were all a seamless continuum. That is truly an ecological art and an ecological poetry.

Menna Elfyn
Libanus, Y Pwll

Gorffennaf, 2006

Cwpons dogni yn ôl,
roedd fy nhad
yn weinidog
yr Efengyl
yn Libanus,
Y Pwll.
Llanelli – chwinciad dur i ffwrdd,
yn ddwy filltir, chwe cheiniog ar y tram.

Ugain mlynedd wedyn,
roedd Libanus
ar y teledu,
Pwll,
yn ddu a gwyn;
sawl gweinidog
yn cyhoeddi,
rhagor na'r 'Gair'.

Ugain mlynedd eto,
hyd at heddiw,
o weinidog i weinidog
a'r 'newyddion da'
yn lludw du.

Dan geseiliau eu tadau,
llu o angylion:
epil ar hap
a'r ddamwain
oedd eu damnio;
o Libanus
i'r Pwll
heb waelod yn y byd.

Lebanon, The Pit

July, 2006

Many ration coupons ago
my father
was a minister
of light
at 'Libanus'*,
'Y Pwll'*,
Llanelli – a blink of steel away,
(two miles, and sixpence on the tran

Twenty years later,
Libanus
was on TV,
The Pit
in black and white,
many a minister
having declaimed
more than the Word.

Twenty years more,
from minister to minister,
to this today,
the 'good news'
blackened to ash.

In the arms of their fathers
a host of angels:
children of chance,
their damnation
an accident,
from Libanus
to Pwll,
the bottomless pit at the end of the v

Cwpons dogni yn ôl
fy chwaer mewn ffrog smoc,
ar wal y Mans
ochr draw i'r fynwent
yn gwylio angladd
ar lan y bedd,
gan gredu'n ddi-ffael
mai pobl-wedi-marw
oedd pob un â hances
yn sychu dagrau;
gêm gyfri oedd marw
i'r un bedair oed;
wrth iddi rifo ugain corff
yn canu 'Dyma gariad'.

Libanus,
Pwll,
meirwon,
heb hancesi,
ar deledu,
yn llawn lliw
eto, yn ddu a gwyn
a sawl gweinidog
heb y Gair 'da'.

Ac ymhell o'r dwndwr,
ymhell o Libanus,
ymhell bell o'r Pwll,
ymhell o lan y bedd,
mae un* mewn cwsg perffaith
heb ei erfyn,

o dan gysur y goleuni clir.

Many ration coupons ago
my sister, in a smocked dress,
sits on the manse wall
watching the churchyard.
She regards the mourners
standing at the graveside,
fully believing
that the people-who-had-died
were those holding the hankies,
wiping tears;
Death was a counting game
for the four-year-old,
as she made out twenty corpses
singing 'O dyma gariad'*.

Libanus,
Pwll,
dead bodies
handkerchiefless
on the news
in full colour
and simultaneous black and white.
Many a minister
without good news.

And far from the tempest,
far from Libanus,
far too from Pwll
or gravesides,
one man* lies in a perfect peace
unsought-for, unasked,

under the solace of a clear light.

Translated by Elin ap Hywel

Wales has many place names taken from the Bible.
* Libanus – Lebanon
*Y Pwll – The Pit
*O dyma Gariad – much-sung hymn, 'O what Love'
*Ariel Sharon

Bernardine Evaristo
Mixing Up The Metaphors

I'm not suggesting that poets of colour* parade outside the Houses of Parliament with banners declaring FREE VERSE! or chain themselves to railings or go on hunger strikes or walk through the streets of London with their supporters singing 'We Shall Overcome' or climb Nelson's Column and set up camp in his hat... now there's a thought. But the issue here is important because poetry is important. It helps shape our understanding of the world, it explores and articulates that which is difficult to express. For many it is oxygen and when some voices are denied air, the effect is, quite simply, suffocation.

I'd known for some time that almost no new poets of colour were getting published in the UK but this hit home when I was a judge on the Next Generation Poets List. Where on earth were the new black and Asian voices – in print? Yes, they excelled at and were encouraged to tread the boards under the razzle-dazzle of the bright lights, but few were invited onto the hallowed pages of a paperback, where poetry is presented as tiny, potent, print, words supported by a spine which bears their name... under the strategic lighting of a bookshop.

It's the complacency that gets me, and the artistic and moral justification from the gatekeepers. How many times have I heard that poetry is so *beyond* politics, so *beyond* narrow definitions of race or culture, so *beyond* everything but the purity of the form. As if poetry is the one aspect of our complex human lives, the one art form, in fact, that exists in a heavenly bubble, devoid of the earthly realities that shape our societies: the hierarchies and power imbalances, the cultural references and preferences, the insider networks with the outsiders looking in.

Instead of donning a suit of antique armour, mounting a horse and getting ready to defend or charge, I hope that the establishment, those in positions of power, read the report with an open mind and seriously consider the question – *what if ?*

* Poets of colour/ Black-Asian poets? OK, no one likes to be labelled but it's shorthand and serves a function in this context.

REVIEWS

℘

[...] grief may continually tell the poet the same thing, but the poet can fight back by responding differently every time.
—*Paul Batchelor on Penelope Shuttle*

The Science Of Possibility

Charles Tomlinson, *Cracks in the Universe*,
Carcanet, £7.95, ISBN 1903039797;
Peter Redgrove, *The Harper*, Cape, £9.00, ISBN 0224077937;
Peter Redgrove, *A Speaker for the Silver Goddess*, Stride,
£8.50, ISBN 1905024169;
Philip Gross, *The Egg of Zero*, Bloodaxe, £7.95, ISBN 1852247266;
Greg Delanty, *Collected Poems 1986-2006*,
Carcanet, £14.95, ISBN 1903039827

A poem's design, or the design of a single poetic line, should suggest possibility, not cast-iron certainty; even though its structure may be as super-involuted as the genetic design of a rose, or an eye. Let a poem carry the argument. This is the entirety of Charles Tomlinson's 'A Rose from Fronteira':

> Head of a rose:
> above the vase
> a gaze widening –
> hardly a face, and yet
> the warmth has brought it forth
> out of itself,
> with all its folds, flakes, layers
> gathered towards the world
> beyond the window,
> as bright as features,
> as directed as a look:
> rose, reader
> of the book
> of light.

The cellular life of a poem is its language, and Tomlinson's language is numinous with life. Alert, evocative, precise language of this standard is not too far from the best observational nature writing, or writing that arises from scientific enquiry. Obviously, a botanist would not reach for the image of the rose as a "reader of the book of light" while writing a paper; but might, were they tilting their findings into creative non-fiction.

Charles Tomlinson is light-years ahead of so many other English poets whose reputations are more visible if less sturdy. Why do we not celebrate him more than we do? It is an old question; and it will not go away. Is he too good for us? *Cracks in the Universe* is a volume brimming with excellences; it extends a body of poetry which has few equals in achievement, perceptual alertness and audacity. I've little doubt that when we look back on poetry from England in fifty years Charles Tomlinson, with Geoffrey Hill and Ted Hughes, will be seen as the figures to reckon with, and to re-read. It is abjectly Little-English to ignore him while he lives – and writes so well – among us. If you are unfamiliar with his work, this book is yet another marvellous place to begin.

Good poetic design engenders possibility. The *oeuvre* of a poet suggests similar strains of possibility. However we tend to read in picks and patches, rather than taking a complete view. It is possible to take that completed view with Peter Redgrove now he has passed on: a scientist and a poet of such range and strangeness that his work arouses as much confusion and talent-blindness among critics as it does curiosity and devotion among readers. I personally feel that, as with Charles Tomlinson, Peter Redgrove is foolishly under-rated but we are beginning to catch up with him at last and, in both cases, that this is our gain.

For some poets, writing poems requires an excess of process in order to create discrimination: their volcano vomits sky-high ash, but there may be a few diamonds scorched into being. This was never Redgrove's project. There is a sense that you need to read his whole output as one long white-hot flow of which these two books are fresh tributaries. Penelope Shuttle quoted that fine critic, the late Philip Hobsbaum in a recent edition of *Stand* as stating, "...the dedicated reader needs to accept Redgrove *en bloc*, demanding though the task may be". Yet Redgrove's work demands only to be read out loud (as Shuttle indicates) for its apparent mysteries to become what they are: open-minded enquiries, clear-eyed explorations.

Personally, I find Redgrove's work beguiling in both its fragments and its wholeness. His balance of science and metaphysical exploration is rigorous and intelligent, alight with parallaxes and possibilities. I was first drawn to his poems because I was a scientist, as was he. But this balance and play of mind has been overplayed by critics who know nothing about science, or who have not grown beyond the image of scientist as anti-imagination empiricist. In my experience, scientists are among the most innovative and lateral workers with language, ideas and images. There is nothing unusual in Redgrove's absolute refusal to stop exploring the inner and outer minds of his worlds; it goes with the training.

What Redgrove knew from the long experience of writing poems is that form must seem inevitable, be near-invisible, a presence in dialogue with the writing. In his later work, he embraced a three-step line; and this allowed him a huge elasticity in voice and pacing. One thing it allows the reader is *speed*: the three-stepped line runs downhill at a clatter. For the poet, the line's shape props and pistons the work forward within the superstructure of a book. Reading Redgrove therefore has never been easier; and both these posthumous collections complete a most remarkable *oeuvre*.

I've admired Philip Gross's poems since his first collection, *Familiars*, in 1983; and never understood why Gross's poetic reputation is not a little more electric, until I discovered that some commentators consider him 'safe', whatever that means. However, one supportive critic commented that Gross's excellence is not just a matter of his imagination but also what he chooses to write about. That goes some way to making a case, but underplays his literary style which is considerable in its linguistic panache. As a poet, Gross can be as experimental and left-field as any self-elected avant-gardist, and in this new collection he plays compendious games with stanza and sound; and also pushes punctuation and numerical marks into open spaces where they begin to sprout into little words and images all by themselves, for example in 'The Channel':

...Our first week apart

I found myself doodling its symbol: brackets
inside-outed. Trust a man
to translate sadness into mathematics

) (

or ink on the page – like opening a *river*
of type, so space might flow...

I was particularly impressed throughout this book by the interplay between line, line-break, various connecting patterns and stanza-shapes; but not distracted to the point where I forgot about the words – the poems indeed – and just enjoyed the technique. Some of the poems are marvellous, not because they are candid, not because they are brave about subject, not even because of the technique on display, but because they are electrifyingly well-observed and beautifully written. Perceptual acuity at this level, like that of Charles Tomlinson, is an act of extreme attention. There is nothing safe or lame in that endeavour; it is one of the hardest of poetic feats.

Lame poems are like lame jokes: they surprise us into boredom. As Greg

Delanty would probably argue, a good joke is itself a decent poem. There is little lame about Greg Delanty's poetry but, in contrast to the sifted compactions of Philip Gross, Delanty creates cocky, wordy, cheerful poems, as well as something we used to call "verse". For purists, any of these gambolling qualities could send a poet to purgatory. Yet good humorous verse is tough to pull off and the best comedy is the thorniest to write.

Within the 'vasty fields' of a complete works, there are bound to be etiolations of poetic energy ("the froth / of goodwill bubbling up like cappuccino" is the kind of image starved by the writer's sheer goodwill). These etiolations occur when Delanty switches all the power from the poem to the *joke* of the poem. Mostly, the wordy bravura keeps the poems alive. By reputation, he is a brilliant performer of his work, and the enlivening syntax of poems such as 'The Natural World' and 'The Shutterbug' wake the ear with their spoken confidence. Of course, all writing *is* performance. Style performs our voice. Our syntax and diction perform language. In Delanty's *oeuvre*, those syntheses are beautifully entangled; messy sometimes, but honest in their occasional clumsiness. In fact, I like this poet a lot more for the faults he shows honestly than for those hidden by technical gloss-paint. Possibility, even the possibility of failure, yields more to the reader than certainty or professionalism.

David Morley's 'Songs of Songs' appears on pp. 18-19.

℘

Swept, Emptied, Kept

ELAINE FEINSTEIN

Eavan Boland, *New Collected Poems*, Carcanet, £ 14.99, ISBN 1857548582;
Muriel Spark, *All The Poems*, Carcanet, £9.95, ISBN 1857548906

Boland is one of the finest and boldest poets of the last half-century. No-one has articulated with more poise the dilemmas of being a woman poet in Ireland. An early feminist, she wrote with her young children around her, finding poetry in early morning bottle-feeds and "woman's secret history" before such concerns were fashionable. She has other powerful themes: emigration, exile, the violence of Irish history, deaths in famine. In her latest books she explores the stoicism of daily life, and the intensities of a long marriage.

Looking back through *New Collected Poems*, it becomes clear that the originality lies in her control of language and tone rather than her own experience. She is one of the few poets able to brush against the vocabulary of late Plath and not lose her own voice. This is because she can make use of Plath's innate surrealism, and extends her metaphors with some wit, for instance in 'Anorexic':

> Flesh is heretic.
> My body is a witch.
> I am burning it.

She understands how women – "swept, emptied, kept" – come to accept the compromises of routine. But her vision of female choices goes deeper. She rages against the Muse of mirrors – "You slut. You fat trout" – and all the female tools used to escape the kitchen and the stink of nappies:

> Eye-shadow, swivel brushes, blushers
> Hot pinks, rouge pots, sticks
> Ice for the pores, a mud mask
> All the latest tricks.

Unlike Akhmatova, say, who trusts her own Muse as unchanging, Boland knows there are many Muses, some of them women writers from other ages. 'The Journey' is one of her most passionate poems. Taking off from that section of the *Aeneid* which describes the crying of unborn babies, Boland is led by Sappho into an Underworld of women from earlier centuries when typhus, cholera, croup and diphtheria ravaged the alleys of old Europe. These are the pains of human experience before antibiotics. Returning to her own life, she reflects:

> If she will not bless the ordinary,
> if she will not sanctify the common,
> then here I am and here I stay and then am I
> the most miserable of women.

In fact it is ordinary detail which gives life to her poetry: a drawer eased by candle grease, or car keys "getting warmer in one hand". She describes what she sees wonderfully – air is "tea-coloured in the garden" – and what she hears: "plum coloured water/ in the sloppy quiet". In her most recent book, she rests her vision of love in daily life:

> I would have said
>> we learned by heart
> the code marriage makes of passion.

Muriel Spark is a novelist of genius – elegant, elliptical, endlessly inventive – who began to publish early as a poet and continued to write poetry all her life. This book deliberately arranges her poems out of chronological order, perhaps to prevent readers peering across too curiously at the novels that run alongside them. (The dates are listed in the Contents.) Nevertheless, several poems evoke the world of Spark novels with precision and charm. The spooky 'Card Party', for instance, has the atmosphere of *The Girls of Slender Means*. And many of her poems have that poignancy, at once knowing and sad, which is the true hallmark of Spark's vision:

> Where does she come from
> Sipping coffee alone in London?
>
> The shoes, the hair – I do not think
> She has anything in the bank [...]

The late poems sometimes abandon that tone of quiet amusement; as in 2000 when she looks back on her own life, across the history of Europe, in 'The Dark Music of the Rue Cherche-Midi'.

Spark is roughly Larkin's generation, and like him has little truck with either American poetry or modernism. Even when she writes with a rhythmic freedom, as in 'Canaan', she likes to use rhyme to make her points:

> Time lacks experience. Therefore I am not quite
> Confounded by history,
> Being of the hopeful race of the earth,
> Promised to promise, a mystery to mystery [...]

In a Foreword written not long before her death she speaks of studying verse forms. Clearly she could write in any form she chose, since she has a fine ear. This volume also includes translations from the Latin of Horace and others. These have a languid lyricism she does not often allow herself elsewhere.

Elaine Feinstein's *Collected Poems and Translations* (2002) was a PBS Special Commendation. *Talking To The Dead* will be published by Carcanet next year.

Variety Show

MATTHEW JARVIS

Simon Armitage, *Tyrannosaurus Rex Versus the Corduroy Kid*,
Faber, £12.99, ISBN 0571233252

In his latest volume, Simon Armitage displays sparkling poetic variety,
delivering work that ranges from the socially engaged to the erudite and
from the deeply serious to the quirky and amusing.

The collection shows its social teeth from the beginning, with the first
piece bearing the dedication *"i.m. Dr David Kelly"*. The poem, called 'Hand-
Washing Technique – Government Guidelines', starts as follows:

1   Palm to palm.
2   Right palm over left dorsum and left palm over right
     dorsum.
3   Palm to palm fingers interlaced.

The reference to David Kelly – the weapons expert whose death in 2003 was
part of the scandal over the British government's assessment of Iraq's
weapons of mass destruction – makes this a poem about escaping political
blame: the hand-washing process that Armitage describes is far more about
a government trying to emerge clean from political difficulties (typified by
Kelly's death) than about scrubbing off physical dirt. Such social awareness
continues with the superb 'KX', which imagines a bomb exploding at a
railway terminal. Thus, the poem urges its "Northerner" addressee to:

> [...]be fleet through the concourse, primed
> for that point in time when the world goes bust,
> when the unattended holdall or case
> unloads its cache of fanaticised heat.

The notion of "fanaticised heat" is powerful, evoking both the bomb
and its social causes. Similarly, in the second stanza, the addressee is "boned
of all thought and sense", an image of violent death which devastatingly
pulls together not only physical destruction but also the elimination of that
which makes a person a thinking, feeling being. The style here is interesting,
too, with the address to "Northerner" and "commoner" making me wonder
whether Armitage has been re-reading early Auden, whose 'The Watershed'

addresses a "Stranger". Indeed, later in this collection, a phrase about the "early empires of lichen and moss" (in the first of two 'Surtsey' poems) is similarly reminiscent of Auden's empires of shark and tiger in 'Spain'.

Armitage's poetic erudition becomes apparent in his renditions of historic poems (*The Odyssey*, 'Sir Gawain and the Green Knight') or – in 'The Bayeux Tapestry' – of cultural artefact. This piece has some similarities with the small-press work of a poet such as Alan Halsey (particularly, perhaps, Halsey's 1995 volume *The Text of Shelley's Death*); and it is testament to Armitage's embrace of poetic variety that such unconventional writing finds a place here:

The(n) nightfall.	Aftermath,
Victory	is a (new) country.
Once battle subsides, a	(numbness) enters the mind.

The poem is divided throughout into two columns. Moreover, its play with parentheses promotes an intriguing sense of textual ambiguity, with the bracketed words being thrown somewhat into doubt. The effect is of a poem taken from a manuscript that has been damaged; or of a work that is especially difficult to translate. By contrast, 'Sir Gawain and the Green Knight' plays no such games. It does, however, offer a splendidly energetic rendition of the fourteenth-century alliterative original. Thus, having been decapitated by Gawain, the Green Knight rides out of Arthur's court:

> With a tug of the reins he twisted around
> and, head still in hand, galloped out of the hall,
> so the flame in the flint shot fire from the hooves.

Just like the Green Knight, it seems, Armitage is a master of display.

That this is a collection with serious intent is apparent early on, with 'On Marsden Moor' contemplating the construction of a "new Jerusalem": not, here, a utopian concept, but rather a grim reflection of present-day Jerusalem as a divided "plot of land". However, there is also humour and oddity throughout the book. 'Republic' imagines a land in which a car's paint-work determines when it may be driven:

> On Tuesdays, white cars alone hit the road.
> Looked at from spy satellites it has snowed.

Amusing though this is, it does seem a little academic: the expression, primarily, of a clever concept. Similarly, although the collection of forty quirky observations which constitute 'Poem on his Birthday' displays some fine lines (such as "The Personnel Department – their collective smirk"), it seems oddly dated, reminding me of a list poem such as Ian McMillan's 'The Twelve Labours of Mr. Cope' from the late 1980s.

It is, however, the first of the five 'Sympathy' poems that causes me most concern. Here, describing the aftermath of a party, Armitage notes an *"Aberfan-meets-Mexican-mudslide toilet bowl"*. Read from Wales, this line feels deeply problematic – notwithstanding the fact that Armitage puts it into the mouth of a far-from-salubrious character. Commenting merely on its Welsh element (and the 1999 Mexican mudslides had the greater death-toll), it is hard to countenance Aberfan being used to create a smart one-liner about a dirty toilet: in 1966, a slag-heap collapsed onto the village and killed 144 people, 116 of whom were children. This line is a disappointing moment, especially in what is generally such an invigorating collection – a collection, moreover, which sets itself so splendidly against the enervating dangers of stylistic uniformity.

Matthew Jarvis is currently working on a book called *Welsh Environments in Contemporary Poetry* (for University of Wales Press).

⁂

Written In Blood

MICHELENE WANDOR

Vicki Feaver, *The Book of Blood*, Cape, £9.00, ISBN 0224076841;
Selima Hill, *Red Roses*, Bloodaxe, £7.95, ISBN 1852247401;
Grace Nichols, *Startling the Flying Fish*, Virago, £8.99, ISBN 1844082911

Lowell, Plath, Sexton have a lot to answer for. Not only were their mid-twentieth-century voices urgent and fresh, not only were their poetics distilled and intense, but they announced in their work the conceptualisation of 'Confessional' poetry. Along with its sacred-secular resonances, combining theology with the practice of psychotherapy, the term also replaced the idea of the 'lyric' with the 'personal' poem, a term now regularly used not just as description, but almost as an implied term of approval. The blurbs of two of these books evoke the latter as a form of praise: Feaver's poems are, supposedly, "intimate personal poems", Nichols apparently writes "of her overseas children".

Of course, in the end (or rather, in the beginning, as one reads the poems) what counts is what poets do or don't do with language, form and content; and one of the interesting legacies of the Confessional 'school' was the trope of bringing into poetry the naming of body parts and elements, particularly blood and bone; as if, perhaps, anatomical precision could help to fix emotional chaos.

The title of Vicki Feaver's third collection is right there: blood in the title, blood capping, as it were, five poems within the first twenty pages or so. Ironically (and somewhat to my relief) the word doesn't appear within the body (*sic*) of the title poem itself. Almost at the end of the book, this is a poem invoking torture, death and filial emotion, using Feaver's great strengths: suggestion, juxtaposition and careful detail. Brutality and beauty share the poetic space. The shock value of the word "blood", when Feaver uses it as a get-out clause to proclaim the end of the poem, undermines the delicacies she has so painstakingly built. The word has become poetically over-determined, a melodramatic device which substitutes for thought.

On a first reading, many of Feaver's poems seem to stop just as they are getting interesting; leading to a comment, perhaps. On second reading, this apparent reservation becomes far less important. The 'blood-bone' cliché ceases to be only that in a line like "his bones like the inside of Maltesers", from a tribute poem to Keats, 'Heat and Cold'; a gem of fine-wrought detail. Here the "blood" is literal, and the word does its own work. The strongest poems are those which accumulate; in 'Horned Poppy', where observation/description allow an almost imperceptible slide into elliptical delicacy at its strongest, as in 'The Trunk'.

Selima Hill's new collection is curious; dedicated "to the men I love", this is a sequence of poems which makes much of plural pronouns. Each poem rhetorically sets a "we" against a "they" in short verbal squibs of plain speaking. Graduate of the school of Emily Dickinson, with a dash of Stevie Smith, this poetic voice has an apparently naïve quality and directness which creates its own rhythms and sets loose frank, not to say sometimes verging on the crude, emotional brickbats. Its plainness produces a paradoxical effect: drawing attention to the message, to the content and import of what is being said, and far less to the way in which it is said. Little imagery, little play with language. The power of the poems lies in their no-nonsense address. But to whom and about what?

Nothing is spelled out or made explicit, but the clues are there in the occasional references: we are back (in part) to the biological; testicles, on the one hand (as it were), and pretty dresses on the other. Though it is nowhere made explicit, men seem constantly on the receiving end of scorn, hate, contempt for rampant sexuality. This radical-feminist assault on the traditionally dominant sex is only half the story, however. There's no compensatory radical-feminist praise of women. Women are weak, pretty, stupid and constantly done over. If there is a linking concept, it is that loving is tough, desirable and impossible. It's the old sex war again. Need for love, and betrayal, are two sides of the same coin in this poetic universe. In a sense this book is the same poem writ over; it's violent and full of fear of the physical. Hate is not converted into satire or analysis. There's no ultimate reason – moral or aesthetic – why it should be. The hate poem has an honourable tradition, but it is one mainly rooted in satire. Although one has to respect the brutal directness, these are like something half-written. But perhaps that is also part of the message: love and sex can only ever be half-written because the collaborators hate each other. Discomforting.

Grace Nichols's new book is like coming into the light. From her first collection in 1983, *I Is A Long-Memoried Woman*, she has been a strong presence in the linguistic interweave between the Caribbean and the UK. Her poetry and prose move easily between the poised world of Western culture, Old World history and myth, and the gritty rhythms of the Caribbean everyday. In this new book, all these preoccupations are present in five sections of untitled poems. Penelope and Zeus from Greek mythology cohabit with Anansi, Mama-Wata from West African myth, Hindu Gods and incantatory names from South America: Inihuatana, Macchu Picchu and Chicomecoatl. The binding in this is the narrative figure of Cariwoma (Caribbean Woman), who draws unto herself the strengths and family fierceness of the Caribbean mother, the wistful exile, a figure who is simultaneously displaced and sure of her belonging.

There is wit, irony and passion; and an integrated, assimilated, absorbed legacy of blood-moon-bone tropes which is exemplary. In a lightly flowing, double-edged coupleted tribute to the Aztecs and the power of their myths, the 'b' word emerges from the rationale built up in the poem to the cumulative envoi: "The blood-carpeted steps of the temple" as a crowning irony of the costs of faith or superstition. Nichols also has a skipping lightness which she keeps in reserve, to bring out with a surprising gloss on a poetic observation of the ordinary: "angels dangling / casual legs" in a garden. It takes real poise to come up with this:

> Zeus, Zeus,
> Whatever happen between us
> Is we business.

Now that's what I call confessional.

Michelene Wandor's *Musica Transalpina*, a PBS Recommendation, is reviewed on pp. 114-115.

Writing By Moonlight

WILLIAM PALMER

Ruth Fainlight, *Moon Wheels*, Bloodaxe, £8.95, ISBN 1852247428

Ruth Fainlight's *Moon Wheels* has thirty-four new poems; translations from Vallejo and other Latin-American poets, and from Sophocles; and selections from two previously published collections.

When men first landed on the moon it was said that its symbolic place in mythology and literature as a mover of tides and emotions, its own mysterious and contrary movements and changes of shape and colour, its cool illumination of lovers, would be forever destroyed; but Fainlight has consistently invoked the moon as a silent witness of our behaviour on earth and as her own "disturbing muse". Here is the first stanza of the title poem 'Moon Wheels':

> The sky is clear and dark, the moon's disk
> far away and small and silver-bright.
> Its cold beam probes through my window:
> the torch of a seeker, invisible
> behind a cone of wavering light.

This seems quite straightforward – until one thinks about the truly eerie and terrifying figure imagined as standing behind the light. The subjects of these new poems range from the tenderly domestic, as in 'The Nest', about finding a pigeon's nest and young, to the horrors of the twentieth century – when 'Crocuses' have

> [...] the almost luminous
> blue and mauve of bruises on the naked
>
> bodies of men, women, children
> herded into a forest clearing
>
> before the shouted order, crack of gunfire,
> final screams and prayers and moans.

– and the continuing horrors of our twenty-first century, where, in 'The Garden of Eden':

> The leaders talk of culture-clash.
> But all cultures might end here,
> where they began [...]

In other poems, images are taken from art and the techniques of painting; in 'A Bowl of Apples' the difficulty of the poet's task is compared to the comparative ease of the visual artist, in that the painter can work simply with the image or abstraction presented to the eye:

> Language
> forces definition. Impossible
> to write a poem impersonal
> as a still life [...]

This is true as far as it goes, but it implies that the painter's task is the easier – though all of us have seen as many mediocre and 'meaningless' paintings as we have read mediocre but 'meaningful' poems. There are a couple of other poems about the difficulty in writing poems too; which may be one too many.

Ruth Fainlight is also a distinguished translator, particularly of the Portuguese poet Sophia de Mello Breyner; and there are some fine examples of that work here. However the most remarkable translations are of a long and fascinating poem, 'Your Hand, My Mouth' by the Mexican, Victor Manuel Mendiola – which might, to paraphrase Wallace Stevens, be called '59 Ways of Looking at a Plate' – and a very powerful version of the suicide of Jocasta and the self-blinding of Oedipus from Sophocles's *Oedipus Rex*.

This leads us to another of Fainlight's preoccupations, with classical mythology. The book reprints eight poems from *Twelve Sibyls*. The fascination of these female prophets – their seat in different cultures from Babylonian to Greek and Roman, their incorporation later into mediaeval Christian mythology, their ability to appear as modern feminist figures and as timeless and powerful sexual icons – means that, in the right hands, they can be an almost inexhaustible source of poetic material. Certainly, the poems printed here are some of the most complex and rich in the book.

This is a fine, varied selection by an important poet who has published many books since 1958. We all know that a *Collected Poems* can look like the tombstone marking the end of a poet's career, but Fainlight deserves the honour and critical attention such an edition would give her. To end with, here is the whole of her sweet, funny and touching poem, 'Never Again':

Old age means not being able
to bite into an apple
walk the length of a valley
see every detail in a pattern
hear the highest alto deepest bass
or wrap my legs around your waist.

William Palmer writes for *The Literary Review* and *The Independent*.

ℬ

Terms For Grief

PAUL BATCHELOR

Penelope Shuttle, *Redgrove's Wife*, Bloodaxe, £8.95, ISBN 1852247347

Why does *Redgrove's Wife* find Penelope Shuttle so eager to dictate terms and conditions to the reader? Take the strangely forthright title (not exactly fearful of being defined in relation to her partner, is she?) or the cover (a picture of a mask called 'La Malinche, interpreter and mistress of Hernán Cortés') or her statement on the back cover regarding the role of the poet (the poet, we are informed, is there to tell us "how to go on loving the world"). The blurb even talks about "life-affirming and redemptive poetry", threatening to re-open a now polarised debate over whether/how/why poetry should offer consolation/support/help in moments of emotional need. It is a relief to see how quickly the work itself escapes such narrow terms: again and again, a title or opening line that promises a direct emotional appeal is subverted into something rich and strange. For example, 'Wife, Widow' begins "Like any married woman, I…" If we are cynical, we brace ourselves at this point for the too-palpable design, the sentimental appeal for easy identification. And then this happens:

Like any married woman
I dream of great houses
disabled by fire,

of maps that grow of themselves,
like old experiments
in organic chemistry

Like any widow
I have a garden
where twelve Apostles and a Christ

dine on mist and rain [...]

The poem takes the form of an extended list of such attributes: some of them come teasingly close to matching their common-sense tone ("Like any married woman / I rank myself below a queen, / above a princess"), but most take pains to frustrate our expectations: "Like any widow I honour the bloodstone, / revere the pearl".

The poems of grieving culminate in 'Missing You,' a moving sequence of twenty-four lyrics which puts Shuttle's trademark invention to service: grief may continually tell the poet the same thing, but the poet can fight back by responding differently every time. Shuttle can be disarmingly direct, and even when she foregrounds poetic devices, her stress on context and the responsibilities of the poet means that the devices never become ends in themselves. This is from 'In the Kitchen':

A jug of water
has its own lustrous turmoil

The ironing-board thanks god
for its two good strong legs and sturdy back

The new fridge hums like a maniac
with helpfulness

I am trying to love the world
back to normal [...]

When grief declares itself as a subject, Shuttle responds with fireworks. Elsewhere, when she considers more diverse subjects (including spiders, postal regulations, endangered languages and driving lessons), she occasionally succumbs to the lure of closure prematurely. It is easy to feel that some of the shorter poems would have yielded even more had Shuttle pursued them further: compare 'Pluvialist' with an earlier gem like 'Taxing the Rain,' which deals with similar subject matter. Like Redgrove's, Shuttle's best poetry tends to work like an accumulator bet: the more sustained the risk, the greater the reward. Conventionally 'important' subject is not a prerequisite: part of the thrill of reading these poets is seeing how their vision transforms the apparently everyday. This is exactly what happens in the best poems of the second half of the book, such as 'Dukedom,' or 'Fountains and Gateways,' where Shuttle allows herself a broad canvas. This is from 'Dukedom':

> He folds me in his septembers worked
> in ivory silk, in his seascapes of living memory.
> He wraps me in his dukedom
> of windfall, goldfinch and peach.
> He inflicts his dukedom on me like dew on a fountain,
> like a year of consents,
> like a lily merchant.

'Footnotes' takes the enough-or-too-much approach into comic territory to good effect, consisting entirely of bizarre footnotes to an unseen, unimaginable text:

> 48. Inventor of the first practical diving bell.
> 49. 'Long may you sleep.'
> 50. A poem of over a million lines describing the destinies of Central Asia from the beginning of time.
> 51. Numerous medical uses of the pigeon.

The fact that English poetry has nostalgic lament as its default setting is an obstacle to the writer who wants to write truthfully about grief and loss. Shuttle rises to the challenge with a confident display of invention which in the hands of a less certain poet would appear tricksy. Instead, Shuttle's insistence on poetry's over-spilling creativity makes a fitting tribute to Redgrove the poet as well as Redgrove the man. Whether the writing of such poetry was therapeutic should not concern us: that Shuttle has designs on the poem rather than the reader ensures the results are genuinely affirming.

Paul Batchelor's pamphlet *To Photograph a Snow Crystal* was recently published by Smith Doorstop.

ℬ

Discursive Humanism

GEORGE SZIRTES

John Haynes, *Letter to Patience*, Seren. £7.99, ISBN 1854114123;
Tim Liardet, *The Blood Choir*, Seren. £7.99, ISBN 185411414X

It was Edgar Allan Poe who argued that long poems are really short poems cobbled together, that the short(ish) lyric *was* the poem. Even now, a romantic instinct suggests that a single heartbeat of sufficient intensity should be enough for both a poem and maybe even a life. Or that the poem at least should act as though that were the case.

In recent years we have seen an increase in the number of books of verse narrative, but there is another form of long poem that is less often explored, that is essentially discursive, taking a theme and conducting a passionate conversation with it, discovering its saying in the process. John Ashbery's 'Self Portrait in a Convex Mirror' is of this sort. Brodsky's 'Lullaby of Cape Cod' is another. The eighteenth century was overflowing with such poems, on cooking, on art, on cider, on philosophy, on criticism. They more or less formed the landscape – in Pope, Johnson and many others in between – but, though Byron loved Pope, Romanticism put paid to them for a good long while.

Now here are two books that are fully thematic; that develop – in their different ways – the complexities of a single experience that is not directly a product of the sensitive lyrical self but of circumstances beyond it. Poems that think and feel their thoughts.

John Haynes's *Letter to Patience*, in consciously Dantesque *terza rima* and divided into Cantos, is a passionate meditation on the memory of some twenty years spent in Nigeria, taking in ideas of empire, personal impressions, personal history, puzzling out the meaning of such an experience given such a history. Liardet's book is the product of time spent as a writer-in-residence in a Young Offenders' prison.

Haynes's is a masterful work of both heart and head. I knew his name a long time ago when it used to appear – or so I think – in Jon Silkin's *Stand* magazine. There is certainly a poem by him in the anthology Silkin edited, the *Penguin Poetry of the Committed Individual*, whose introduction tried to lay out some kind of manifesto for what Silkin considered to be 'committed.' The book appeared in 1973, by which time Haynes (not to be confused with the American poet John Haines, who is also in the anthology) was already teaching in Nigeria.

Letter to Patience begins by precisely locating the writer in England in 1993, he having returned from Nigeria with his Nigerian family to nurse his dying father; and the poem, like the *Commedia*, covers a specific number of hours in the writing, to daybreak. This having been established in the Preface and the first Canto, Haynes quickly lodges the reader in Patience's village bar in Northern Nigeria, with: "[...] a road, a row / of houses with the horns and plasticine- / like joins of walls, as if the radio // is wrong, or here has not been touched[...]". The poem then moves back and forward in time trying to make sense of the relationship between the author's heart and mind and the long years in Nigeria.

The letter-writer, we understand, went out to Nigeria in the wake of late sixties radicalism, attuned to Silkin's ideas but fully his own man. What he reads into Nigerian life is the history of colonialism and capital. If it stopped there this would still be a fascinating book but it would not be poetry. Although he brings a substantial theoretical apparatus to bear on the personal with all its apparent contradictions, the driving forces of the poem are the affections and the senses as applied through thought:

> What is it to meet someone? What is it
> to see the huge real eyes of them? To bawl
> out of each others' baby brains and quite
>
> all sense of who gazes and who's seen, all
> hissing skin and hissing hands that slow,
> slow, slow away to breath, to air, landfall
>
> at last [...]

One short passage, as ever in reviews, must serve as entry to a whole poem, but the key is here, human, tangible, capable of deep feeling, understanding, interpretation and intellectual wonder at the same time. *Letter to Patience* is a marvellous book, an exemplar of sorts; as for the virtuosity it is entirely at the service of the vision.

Credit also to Seren for publishing Tim Liardet's *The Blood Choir*, a series of poems written while Liardet was teaching at a Young Offenders' prison. I have occasionally thought the initiative of putting poets in such places was a rather artificial exercise, the poem produced straining after a deeper comprehension of something with which they had had rather fleeting contact, in other words almost a kind of empathetic betrayal.

Ken Smith's book *Wormwood* (1987), produced out of a period as resident writer at Wormwood Scrubs prison, showed it need not be like that and so does Liardet's. Liardet refuses to speak *for* – meaning *in place of* – the young imprisoned men, to employ them for broad rhetorical purposes or as sounding boards for his own sensibility. Liardet works with them and allows them the space that their physical circumstances cannot afford. He listens, he registers, he trains his ear to hear them in the dark, he occasionally registers his own registering, but throughout the book he is engaged in a truthful, intense effort in describing and comprehending the humanity in them as well as their place in humanity.

And some of it is uncomfortable and clearly a shock to him, but he perseveres and keeps his eyes open, never sentimentalising. In a short poem 'Shoe Gazing' he poses the balance between himself and them quite beautifully:

> [...] They have found my new shoes
> and squabble, trying to read the label.
> Into their white-as-sea-foam trainers,
> earned for good behaviour, I slip an overcautious foot.

The respect and astonishment of seeing those "white-as-sea-foam trainers" is worth a hundred sermons on man's inhumanity to man or on the nature of innocence. It is not a sermon: it is a discovery that arrives at the window of the imagination much as the sea suddenly does.

It is these sudden openings out, following on the claustrophobia of routine and expectation, that are most remarkable. In another poem, 'Spaniels in a Field of Kale', two dogs offer a vision of freedom that begins in a field but does not stop there:

> The logic of them flopping and collapsing, flies
> out in a northerly direction towards the last outcrops
> of Scapa Flow, or keeps going with the rafts
> of over-rushing altocumulus due west
> to the land floes of Inishbofin, east to Orford Ness
> or south to the lip of the Lizard, where it hovers panting
> over the odd ellipsis of Land's End [...]

having offered which the poem returns at the end to:

> [...] a sort of flowing yolk built around
> the features of a little prune face
> and mouthful of yappy snarls.

It is perspective that adds depth, a sort of historical-psychological depth of field, to both Haynes's and Liardet's books. This is certainly Liardet's best book to date. It is what poetry is for: to register life, to turn it back into life through language. It is a part of the humaneness of both books that they don't just respond but *think* about the bit of life they hold in their hands: they tell us how it feels but also how it got there and where else it belongs.

George Szirtes won the 2005 T. S. Eliot Prize for *Reel*.

❧

Forms Of Sentience

KIT FAN

Chase Twichell, *Dog Language*, Bloodaxe, £8.95, ISBN 185224738X;
Elizabeth Alexander, *American Blue: Selected Poems*,
Bloodaxe, £8.95, ISBN 1852247304;
Tomaž Šalamun, *Row*, Arc, £9.95, ISBN 1904614094

Towards the end of *The Ghost of Eden* (1995), Chase Twichell captures a thrilling encounter with the "God-eyes of the fishercat" that "were empty of / any language I could extract." Eleven years later, in *Dog Language*, she writes in 'Soul in Space': "I want my obituary to say that / I wrote in the language of dogs". Bringing together the Tower of Babel and Jack's Beanstalk, she imagines words as seeds and pages as ladders, but doesn't want to sit "sprinkling / black letters on a white ladder, / leading my own eye down". Stranded on that ladder, we don't know whether the poet is on the way up or down. At the end, or the beginning, of this vertiginous journey, the poem ends as the poet realizes "the dog was gone". The wonderfully dreamy and allegorical poem is just one of many instances in Twichell's search for a language with "its own distinctive / form of sentience".

In 'Work Libido' Twichell lays out the rules of sentience: "*Tell the truth. No decoration. Remember Death*". *Dog Language* is indeed haunted by many deaths. The book opens with a post-war 'Skeleton': "Look at the skull" the speaker says, "I'm its voice". Images of bones scatter through the childhood poems, taking us back to 'The Paper River', "full of driftwood and detritus, / bones hung with trinkets" and to the roe found inside a trout as the poet's father breaks its spine. The stark elegies for Twichell's father, in 'Hail and Farewell', record his gradual decline without sentimental "decoration": this elegiac sequence is as powerful as Douglas Dunn's *Elegies* or Penelope Shuttle's 'Missing You'. In 'The Soup', for example, Twichell presents a disturbing connection between life and food:

> I went to see Dad at the Home.
> The soup was turkey corn chowder
> with wild rice. Not bad, considering
> we ate it in the waiting room
> of the house of death.

The "we" connects the "I", "Dad", and "us", the reader. In *Dog Language* Twichell finds a fine equilibrium between the fierce, apocalyptic elegies of *The Ghost of Eden* and the dreamy meditations of *The Snow Watcher* (1999). For three decades she has risked creating a new poetic for each book, like Jorie Graham. While searching for her imaginary "dog language" she recaptures the peculiarity of real human utterance, making us recognize the force of her claim that "Our words should cauterise / all wounds to the truth". This is Twichell's most compelling and intimate collection to date.

While Twichell is drawn to the language of animals, Elizabeth Alexander breezily defines her poetry in terms of the "human voice":

> Poetry (and now my voice is rising)
> is not all love, love, love,
> and I'm sorry the dog died.
> Poetry (here I hear myself loudest)
> is the human voice.

This sense of poetic immediacy runs through *American Blue*, a reverse-chronological selection from four US collections: *Venus Hottentot* (1990), *Body of Life* (1996), *Antebellum Dream Book* (2001) and *American Sublime* (2005). Drawing on black history, politics, art exhibitions and music, Alexander summons past and present human voices to explore the internal estrangement of being black in America. In her essay 'The Black Interior' (published here as a coda), she argues that black artists "are often prisoners of the real, trapped in fantasies of 'Negro authenticity'", something that "exists for a mainstream audience" and "their fantasies for our authentic-ness". To counter this and respond to the demand of the "real", Alexander resorts to an idea of "the black interior", an "inner space" of spawning dreamscapes where selves "go far beyond the limited expectations and definitions of what black is, isn't, or should be".

Her poems often tune into real human voices but take off on dreamy riffs of their own: a "Negro crooner" reinterprets Nat King Cole's 'Eskeemos', the poet fetches the Nobel novelist "a Starbucks / macchiato grande, with turbinado sugar" in 'The Toni Morrison Dreams', Sylvia Plath sets the poet's hair "on rollers made from orange-juice cans", Pablo Neruda discusses "a better language / for poems", and the poet dreams of Nelson Mandela tending a garden "on a rooftop of a prison". Alexander's famous, playful, incestuous cast-list combines realistic materials with exhilarating dream-work, creating a fantastical fissure between the imaginary and the real, where she articulates her poetic concerns for racial and sexual inequality, poverty and exploitation. Though she casts herself as public spokesperson, many poems speak with intimacy and humour, as for example she recalls "one hundred megawatts of butter" consumed in her childhood. *American Blue* is a glittering showcase for Alexander's poetic performances of the last decades.

Reading Tomaž Šalamun's second UK selection, *Row,* is like pleasurably browsing among the shelves of Borges's 'The Library of Babel'. In 'White Hash, Black Weed, Gregor is Telling Me What You are Doing?' – a firework display of international places and people, published in *Poetry Review* 96:2 – the poet announces, "I don't invent. I don't lie. I don't exaggerate", as if this were the 11th Commandment. The reader is perplexed and excited by Šalamun's persona, as much as those three seriously mischievous verbs, which mock confessionalism, propaganda, dogma, mythology, and of course, the poetic self.

Introducing Šalamun's previous UK selection, *Homage to Hat and Uncle Guido and Eliot* (1988), Robert Hass underlines his "eclecticism", his "sense of improvisation", "the surrealist lists, the New York School fast jottings of what's going on at the moment, the disjunctions, and sense of play". While Šalamun's risky, experimental poetics reflects his interests in Williams, O'Hara and Ashbery, the landscapes and events in the poems recall other Eastern European poets such as Herbert, Holub, Milosz and Zagajewski. For example, in 'Rituals and the Little Skin' in *Row*, after a fanfare of disjunctive and evocative images, Šalamun ends with a war-scene: "The world is dripped on with dew. They chained / the river Soča. I'm called to the soldier's ground. There / I will shave files. Before every lunch and after every birth." The present tense brings back past wars, as the Soča Valley was the stage of major military operations in WW I where over 300,000 lost their lives. Šalamun's surrealistic worlds are often inhabited by real history, defining a space where inventions, lies, exaggerations, and their opposites contest each other.

Kit Fan is finishing a thesis on Thom Gunn. His poems have appeared in *Poetry Review, The Rialto* and *Acumen.*

Landscapes Of The Imagination

JUDITH KAZANTZIS

Michelene Wandor, *Musica Transalpina*, Arc, £8.95, ISBN 1904614256;
Imtiaz Dharker, *The Terrorist At My Table*, Bloodaxe, £8.95,
ISBN 1852247355; Janet Sutherland, *Burning The Heartwood*,
Shearsman, £8.95, ISBN 139780907562887; Helen Ivory, *The Dog In The Sky*,
Bloodaxe, £7.95, ISBN 1852247177

Here are four very different and seductive landscapes of the imagination. *Musica Transalpina* in particular has a depth of historical and cultural understanding unusual in contemporary British poetry. It is a homage both to the Renaissance and to Michelene Wandor's other arts, the theatre and chamber music. Here, her dramatic narratives take on an age where great paintings and music filled palaces while plague decimated the poor. As in previous work, Wandor weaves in and out of her palaces and artists a counter strand: Jewish women, in an anti-Semitic Europe, become her hidden heroines.

Dramatic narrative gives full play to Wandor's gifts for counterpoint, collage and the undervalued power of understatement. The spare is set against the flowing: the lines evoke both the King James Bible and the song rhythms of Renaissance artifice. Antithesis is at the core. The title poem, 'Musica Transalpina', brings grandeur to one tragic (modern) example. An Italian cable-car, like a "ladybird", falls down the mountain; nature, the Alps, are for a moment gleefully destructive, then spookily, sunnily indifferent. Back in time, the story of Biblical Esther, sung like a broken fairytale, opposes human tyranny against the language of freedom. The book's most original piece, 'Emilia's Poem', spins such matters into an sly, quizzical, Tudor fantasia: could one Emilia Bassano Lanvier, possibly a Marrano (a secret Jew), historically an English woman poet, have been Shakespeare's Dark Lady?

Emilia's virtual tale contrasts with the solid gold historical ego of the great Benvenuto Cellini, whose famously self-satisfied *Life* is retold with a witty eye for scholarly detail. What keeps these lines so taut, not sunk by scholarship? Michelene Wandor is a mistress of ironies. Her shifting refrains tease the sensuous against the dry and the hinted; on the one hand look for the bitten-off comment, on the other enjoy her rich and sensuous inventories. Essentially it is the play between the official and the ironic, resistant voice that makes this such a rewarding book: a paradoxical theatre, private and public, absorbing and suddenly powerful.

The landscapes of Imtiaz Dharker's second collection are also about contrast, as she pans deftly across East and West. After an immigrant childhood in Glasgow, her adult life flies her constantly between London and Mumbai. Where is home in all these landscapes? And what of other places? Chopping onions rings in her kitchen, Dharker sees Gaza like "a spreading watermark" under her fine tablecloth. Elsewhere she says, "We float without time. / The whole of London is our present / sent to us in battered envelopes / postmarked Srinagar, Ramallah, Grosny". Uncertainty threads the whole book with cool ambiguous tension. Entering history, the poetic voice is simpler, vivid: recreating 'Lascar Johnny', the Indian merchant seamen who became pedlars in the Scottish Highlands. In 'Remembering Andalus', that lost Moorish state, the verse rises to the architectural poetry of the Alhambra with almost effortless sensuousness, utterly unsentimental:

> These things will not be trapped
> in marble, the moon in water
> has never been the same before or since.

Then we are back in today's world, especially Mumbai and its streets: noisy, irresistibly alive. The last sequence, *World Rickshaw Drive*, solves Dharker's existential doubts by kidnapping her on a Mumbai autorickshaw. The "mad Mogul rickshaw driver" is no Virgil; but his splendid unstoppability brings Dharker's journeying to a satisfactory "halfway". Behind giant advertising screens, which rear like the stone faces of a frightening myth, she discovers only "my neighbour, my sister. // The grace of the familiar. / The blessed. / The everyday". In the final poem, 'Halfway', she enters an epiphany of singing crowds. As for politics, "Men stumble from the sea / with giant flags, wind-whipped. / Children climb over a stone head. Whose?" And so:

> We navigate this fractured time
> consulting ancient maps,
> overtaking on the autoroutes
> the unicorn, the poet king.
>
> Halfway home or halfway gone,
> we have grown accustomed now
> to travelling on the faultline
> of daily miracles.

In *Burning the Heartwood*, Janet Sutherland's comment on the world is much terser. Starting from Darwin, "From so simple a beginning / Endless forms /Most beautiful /Spin out −" she surveys the result: "Famine and death / Surround us / We march on". Brief, eloquent lines speak of a personal world of growing things, gardens, women, love, endurance. Her poems are questioning, tender, guarded; the poet knows that what is told is "less than a fraction / of what really happens"; nevertheless a day of women talking together means more than just endurance: "there was joy in the recognition / and learning to care / is the other thing". Love poems mingle with fine nature poems. In the subtly-paced 'Four Different Kinds Of Water', the poem ranges freely from a downland Adonis Blue to love itself: "sea accepts / her skin is more or less water / finds the creases under breasts [...]". Like Imtiaz Dharker, finally the poet seeks a home − which may be in the downs and the sea:

> [...]a place to be aimed for
> with warmth
> moss from a damp wood, yellow tormentil
> chalk shining in the broad light
> of wind, taken up
> drawing the mind to its den
> of silence.

Finally for something completely different. *The Dog In The Sky* twitches the dark; lighthearted personae playful against a cosmic shiver. Any surrealism relies at bottom on a certain passionate madness, which Ivory doesn't always sustain; sometimes her language is too easy, a sweet-toothed Gothic. But between the play, a woman is helpless with love, a couple circles edgily, the children are soon to be told lies (here the villanelle is just the right form). Ivory's uneasy little hero dog is suddenly lost − shame! − shot up into the fear and the ecstasy of space and the stars. In the midst are poems like 'Listen Only To Your Breathing', where love's inventory excludes the ubiquitous small animals and needs only a room and clouds. Back 'In The Glass Room',

> her words were tiger-moths [...].
> He spoke laughing birds;
> they gobbled up some
> tigermoths
> while chortling to themselves.
> She cried snowflakes [...]

The tension is real, splendid: then, glued too firmly into the surreal, it dissipates – as elsewhere – in a chorus of bad creatures "gleefully" chortling (or good ones "giggling"). On the other hand, love's withdrawal, in 'The Disappearing', is feeling and ethereal, while 'Persona' is memorable about a highly existential werewolf. In the end erotic love lives and lives hard, as in 'Miscible', with its (justified) sliver of Ann Sexton:

> Talk to me in rainfall, think of me as a riverbed
> in the heat of summer; empty, baked, longing[...]

> Come, my pretty – there is nothing to stop you now.
> The small fishes of my hands are waiting to greet you[...]

Judith Kazantzis's 'The Dose' appears on p. 51.

❧

Small Press Round-Up

NIGEL MCLOUGHLIN

Katrina Porteus, *Longshore Drift*, Jardine Press, £10.00, ISBN 0953947297; Tobais Hill, *Nocturne in Chrome & Sunset Yellow*, Salt, £8.99, ISBN 1844712621; Peter Finch, *The Welsh Poems*, Shearsman, £9.95, ISBN 0907562914; Constance Short & Tony Carroll (comp.), *Eddie's Own Aquarius*, Cahermee Publications, £20.00, ISBN 0955158400; Andy Croft & Cynthia Fuller (eds.), *North by North-East*, Iron Press, £10.00, ISBN 090622893X; David Kessel, *O the Windows of the Bookshop Must Be Broken: Collected Poems 1970–2006*, Survivor's Press, £8.00, ISBN 1874595062; Hugh Purcell (ed.), *We're Going On! The Collected Poems of Tom Wintringham*, Smoke Stack, £6.99, ISBN 0955106109; Adonis, Mahmud Darwis, Samih al-Qasim, *Victims of a Map: A Bilingual Anthology of Arabic Poetry*, SAQI, £9.99, ISBN 0863565247; *Into Glasgow*, Mariscat Press, £6.00, ISBN 0946588201; *Handmade Fire*, Malika's Poetry Kitchen, £4.00, ISBN 1905233108

Katrina Porteus's book *Longshore Drift* is a beauty. With its hard-back, its dust-cover and James Dodds's striking illustrations, it looks and feels like books should. Inside, there is an experiment in progress: getting a poem which is read in two voices and which has overt dramatic qualities to lend itself to paper. It's problematic. Something has been lost in the attempt and I felt that the inclusion of a CD might have been a good idea. That is no slight on the poetry. The poem itself is very fine indeed and uses its voices singularly well by allowing them to play off and weave around each other. I'd just love to hear it performed with full sound effects. Porteus's pared-down poetry has all the resonance of the dissonant, sibilant and bleak environment she evokes:

> The small boats face the waves
> Their broad, white clinker curves
>
> A cockle's ripped shell –
> Something the sea has made.

It is perhaps significant that Porteus, a native of Aberdeen, sets her poem in Aldeburgh, where the dialect she hears distances her from a way of life she admits feeling connected to. She is able to transfer this sense of alienation and estrangement to the reader, both through vocabulary and diction and through her use of the dramatic elements of voice.

Tobias Hill has already established a reputation as one of the best poets writing. *Nocturne in Chrome & Sunset Yellow* will do that reputation no harm at all. The central sequence of the book, 'A Year in London', is an impressive series of snapshots in which the voice is urbane and relaxed; the tensions have all been transferred to language and line:

> yards like cesspits, and everywhere carnivals
> of people, the crowds embracing their collision.

The prose poem 'December' is among the best of the sequence. The language is taut and rattles along with a consonantal energy generated by a preponderance of 't' and 'k' sounds which give the poetry an abrasive texture:

> The air is pricked
> with awns of ice that settle in my two-week beard. A man on the
> bench by the ginkgo tree hunkers down against the cold.

The other poems in the book sustain the level set by that central sequence. Startling images creep up on the reader unawares:

> Hold tight. There's good in us, as there is
> inside the sharp, green hulls of the chestnuts,

> which open as we tread them underfoot,
> halving to reveal themselves, not cold,
> or spent, but bright as bloody, beating hearts.

Let's face it, these poems are simply very, very good.

Peter Finch's *The Welsh Poems* frustrated me! I wanted to grab them by the throat and shake sense out of them – but perhaps that's exactly what Finch intends to confer; that feeling of being lost and frustrated in a sea of disobedient language which never does what you want (or expect) it to do whether you're writer or reader or both. I admit I was much more comfortable in his less abstract pieces which allow the reader at least a foothold in the sometimes sheer landscape of his language. At times he startled me with proto-metaphors that emerged from the text as if untouched:

> foliage not knocked back
> by frost like our voices
> we have to speak we sing
> no tune

Other times, I was much less comfortable: the 'Dauber' poems and the 'Composition Theory' poems left me cold, asking myself why the reader should care enough to struggle with them. But I *did* struggle, so perhaps Finch achieved his aim. Maybe his intention is to leave his reader floundering in wilderness. There is something oddly likeable about the first half of the book where he works "the oven / with its roaring fan and gargled heat" to produce a language which melts and liquefies in the grasp; but which poses serious questions about our understanding of that language and about what the power relationships between us and the word really are.

Sebastian Barker once asked *Who is Eddie Linden?* This *festschrift* for the great man, *Eddie's Own Aquarius*, goes a long way to answering that question. At 172 pages it's a thumping good read, full of small fragments and snippets of who or what Eddie Linden is. One can saunter through this book as one might an art gallery, stopping where one's eye is drawn to consider intriguing pieces. The contributors list reads like a Who's Who of the literary scene, but more importantly there is genuine affection for, and celebration of, the man in these pieces. From their range one gets a picture, not directly of, the man, but of the love and respect he can inspire. In the words of one of Eddie's own poems, "only in the gallery will you find the finished piece / and find the man."

North by North East covers forty-nine poets in 377 pages. If you want to know what's going on right now in the poetry scene in the North East, this is the book to buy. Like all good anthologies, it offers the reader a chance to discover poets they hadn't previously read. Among those who impressed me are Kevin Cadwallender and Valerie Laws. Cadwallender's poems speak from the inner city and the voice has a knowing humour which lifts the poems above their bleak surroundings. Laws's images are vivid and the language rattles and sparks. One gets the feeling she chooses her subjects carefully, seeking the intense and the pregnant within them and offering the reader something of the 'real' experience they contain. Of course the anthology also offers generous selections of work by Harrison, Stevenson, Allnutt, Herbert, O'Brien *et al*; as well as the excellent Brendan Cleary, S.J. Litherland and Katrina Porteus.

Also in the post-bag this time around were five further volumes of note. David Kessel's *O The Windows of the Bookshop Must Be Broken* collects poems from thirty-six years of writing by a survivor of mental illness. In Hugh Purcell's selection of work by Tom Wintringham, *We're Going On!*, the poems are very much of their time and form an interesting historical document. The anthology *Victims of a Map* consists of translations from three Arab poets and although the poems are interesting in terms of theme and subject, the English translations seem rather stilted and unnatural. *Into Glasgow* presents translations of, and responses in Glaswegian to, poets from Shakespeare and Catullus to Issa and William Carlos Williams. *Handmade Fire* is an anthology of work from a 'writing community'. It contains some achieved work and I will be keeping a weather eye out for more from many of those included.

Nigel McLoughlin's *Blood* (2005) was published by bluechrome. He is Field Chair in Creative Writing at the University of Gloucestershire.

ℬ

Daisy Chain

STEPHEN KNIGHT

Kate Bingham, *Quicksand Beach*, Seren, £7.99 ISBN 1854114115;
Tishani Doshi, *Countries of the Body*, Aark Arts, £9.99, ISBN 1899179070;
Jenny Joseph, *Extreme of Things*, Bloodaxe, £8.95, ISBN 1852246812

Quicksand Beach, Kate Bingham's polished second volume, is a daisy chain of connections: an angry mother is imagined as a lion in one poem, and on the next page the real beast appears amidst domesticity as "a stink in the kitchen"; 'His Eyes', which ends with a man awake in bed, is followed by 'Hypnagogia', a fine evocation of the world of the sensitized insomniac:

> dim-cabined aeroplanes fly in one ear
> and out the other, sirens twine from far to near,
> a taxi stops, drunk women shout good-bye,
>
> someone walks home with change in his pocket.

One thing leads to another, and strangeness and unease slowly emerge after some predictable forays into childhood, marriage, pregnancy and motherhood. One of the six words repeated in all three of the collection's sestinas, "love" recurs at regular intervals, though it is a love full of disquiet. A sign that all is not cosy arrives with the twelfth poem, 'Gale Force Ten', when "The wind wanted everything to be flat / so I lay down on the pavement." Instability in the home is examined in 'Breath', in which a husband insists he is happy in spite of his sleeplessness; and another bad night is followed by the sun "filtering through something like snow /on the window." One of the book's other motifs, snow chills the atmosphere, falling out of season or, in the unnerving 'In the Birchwood', gradually filling a hat which belongs to the poem's speaker, who has narrated his own suicide.

Read from beginning to end as a quasi-narrative, which is perhaps Bingham's intention (the book opens with a piece about imminent motherhood and closes with one about the speaker's first home, "my cot in the stable beyond repair"), *Quicksand Beach* can be a little disappointing. The quotidian poems at either end are no match for the heightened poems at its heart. The expository material of the fourth of the 'Roads' sonnets, for example – "At services I climb out after you / and hang about in ugly striplight / holding the petrol cap as if to help us / be quicker" – would seem dull even in the more forgiving climate of a novel. Formal variety provides some balance, though poems based so closely on episodes from life always risk prosiness, even when handled by a writer as adept as Kate Bingham. It isn't that her versification becomes splashy halfway through, but that the disjunction between unshowy style and bizarre content gives rise to curious details and vertiginous perspectives. When *Quicksand Beach* dramatises uncertainty it begins to fulfil the promise of its title.

Kate Bingham's well-mannered vignettes of suburban life, their low-key details and phlegmatic rhythms, are quintessentially British. Born in India (though widely travelled), Tishani Doshi is a different kind of writer altogether. The unusual choice of verb in the first sentence of her debut, *Countries of the Body*, announces an ambition to surprise:

> The day we went to the sea
> Mothers in Madras were mining
> The Marina for missing children.

Doshi's poetry is full of evocative atmospheres and vivid imagery; hunched men are "curved / Like farm tools", hotel soap is "a tiny rectangle / In the heart of [a] hand", aunts are "Grown maritally large / Like watermelons". Her images elide surreally one into the other, often to haunting effect, and her unabashed Romanticism is refreshing.

However, the slipperiness of Tishani Doshi's poetry, its occasional opacity, is both a virtue and a weakness, and not only because of a uniformity of attack over a full-length collection. Doshi at times seems to be as intoxicated by her voice as she is in control of it. Punctuation is erratic – she often uses full stops where commas would be appropriate – and grammar is imprecise: men are "In overalls and grizzly chests and meaningful / Silences" ("in" grizzly chests?); a pleasing but oddly phrased image has the girls of 'Love in Carlisle' "Holding each other up like poles of wilted beanstalks"; and a woman is heard "Beating her retarded boy for smoking cigarettes / With the stray end of a coconut branch", which is a novel way to take a drag. Phrases in the text – "We must make meaning of things", "a dissolved mess", "garbled pieces" – come to read like comments on it. This waywardness is frustrating because Tishani Doshi's talents are evident throughout *Countries of the Body*. Rigorous editing would have picked up the lapses as well as questioning some of the poetry's other tropes (like the over-insistent alliteration of the volume's first sentence, quoted above).

Based on a painting by Gwen John, the opening poem of Jenny Joseph's

Extreme of Things is plain and mysterious:

> The house is very still and it is very quiet.
> The chair stands in the hall: lines on the air;
> Bar back, a plane of wood, focus in a space
> Polished by dusk and people who might sit there.

One of that exceptional generation of writers which includes Ted Hughes, Sylvia Plath and Geoffrey Hill, Jenny Joseph knows how to manage a line of poetry, and knows when to use and when not to use particular effects. The strangely potent deliberateness of the first line, the unexpected triple rhyme, the enjambed third line drawing out that rhyme 's arrival, and the appearance of notional people in the last line all make for a memorable piece of writing.

A new and selected (the latter chosen for their "elemental happenings and changing seasons"), *Extreme of Things* is haunted by children and child-like voices. Joseph has included poems written for younger readers, so the book's timbre along with its motif of the passing seasons result in an understated poignancy. For those readers familiar with Jenny Joseph only through her celebrated 'Warning', this latest collection's Prufrockian ambience – "the light struggles down brown passages of air", "For at our dying, unclenching the hand all that we find there / Is 'Does it matter if we know?'" – and its ambition will be revelatory. Of the nineteen new poems, the plainest are also the most striking. 'The magic of the brain', 'Lullaby' and 'Exody' are all better than 'Warning', though their author might not thank me for saying so.

Stephen Knight's *Sardines and Other Poems* (Young Picador) was published in 2004.

ℬ

"I remember as a young writer

a great sense of gratification at

being included in **POETRY**,

of being admitted to some surer

order of the art." *Seamus Heaney*

ENDPAPERS

❧

[...] a poet must be willing to be a little stupid
and a little reckless.
—Chase Twichell

LETTER FROM THE ADIRONDACKS

CHASE TWICHELL

As the editor of an independent literary press (Ausable Press, founded in 1999), I read a great deal of poetry that is looking for a home. Because the Press accepts unsolicited submissions in June of each year, and anyone writing in English may submit a manuscript (we receive an average of five hundred each year), it has been useful to me to try to articulate exactly what it is I am and am not looking for. This is actually quite difficult, as it of course applies to my own work as well.

We receive everything from science fiction sagas to Great Aunt Elsie's sonnets, but the vast majority of books that cross my desk are well-crafted, earnest, serious, literate works that have few or no overt flaws, and yet do not move or excite me. These books are often the product of our flourishing MFA industry (the degree is now offered by several hundred colleges and universities). Each year approximately a thousand new volumes of poetry, in the form of the required MFA thesis, begin the search for a publisher. While there's always the exception, the majority of these books simply lack certain qualities I insist on, both as a reader and poet: a book has to tell the truth and it has to be as least as smart as I am. I need to feel in the presence of a human consciousness from which I can learn, and I want that mind to speak to me of profound matters in language made new to me.

Most poems I read have not yet tracked their truths into the ground. Instead, they do other work: they explore and describe emotion; they compose linguistically musical scores; they analyze and archive experience. But every once in a great while I open a manuscript and a voice speaks to me, precisely and without embellishment, about sentience. That excites me. I hop out of my chair and read the rest of it pacing up and down my study. Such poems seem to come from a kind of egoless mind like the mind of meditation. I've seen it in young and old poets alike. It's rare, but unmistakable, even if still innocent, and might be defined as a profound curiosity unfazed by failure. In order to write poems that cross into the mysteries of love and death and return with something freshly discovered in language, a poet must be willing to be a little stupid and a little reckless, and to confront repeatedly his endless ignorance and fear, his vanity, cowardice, and laziness. The pursuit of truth is difficult and mostly thankless work. It's also the most important thing a human being can do on this poor blighted planet, so close to the world's end.

EDITORIAL

FIONA SAMPSON

The theme of this issue seems designed to make us look both inwards, at ourselves, and outwards, at the world affairs we increasingly view through its lens.

Identity is the theme for this year's National Poetry Day, on October 5th; and it's an important, fertile one, as this extra-full *Poetry Review* shows. But what starts with a sense of celebrating each "I in my intricate image", as Dylan Thomas has it, is quickly shadowed by the question – whose image? And how much do we own the (other) things we imagine? At the time of writing, the world's eyes are once again on the Middle East. But, as Menna Elfyn's contribution to *"Representative Writing"…?* shows, what's 'over there', viewed from Llandysul or London, is also 'over here'; and of course vice versa. As Elfyn says, "Bethlehem, Nasareth, Nebo… we are loaded with them in Wales… And Libanus [Lebanon] to me always meant Llanelli". In a country overwritten by the Christian narrative, many place-names are Biblical; for the child growing up in Wales, Jericho and Sion simply *are* made of grey nineteenth-century slate – and rain. The imaginary, like the self, is created through negotiation, conflict and in context. Viewed this way, all naming, and all writing, is part of a continuing – a life-long – process of self-invention which, horror-stories about poetic egos aside, is our most serious, and socially-responsive, task.

Elsewhere in this issue, therefore, Hélène Cixous finds her way out of Algeria and into a relationship with the US through reading, research, writing. John Burnside reads across the Atlantic and – in an echo of *Resurgence* editor Satish Kumar's essay on 'Representing the Landscape' – reads the American relationship to landscape in the poetry of Brigit Pegeen Kelly. And Chase Twichell reminds us that reading, like writing, may be a search for the astonishments of the human.

One of the other features of this issue of *PR* is a series of versions of poets living and dead – Cavafy, Dante, Tranströmer – alongside our usual original poetry and translations. Versioning, that complex negotiation of at least two poetic identities (poet's, translator's and, sometimes, the poet's pre-existing reputation in the host language), brings both writer and reader very close to that fundamental question of writing identity, Who do I write *as*?

Who do we *read* as?

CONTRIBUTORS

Patience Agbabi – page and stage, highbrow and lowbrow – finds opposites attract and is currently working on a third collection, *Bloodshot Monochrome*.

Nazand Begikhani is a much anthologised Iraqi Kurdish poet. Her recent *Colour of Sand* (Erbil, Iraq, 2005) was co-written with Dilawer Qaradaghi.

Beverley Bie Brahic has translated several of Hélène Cixous's books. Her collection *Against Gravity* was published by Worple in 2005.

Eavan Boland's *New and Collected Poems* was published this year. This poem was first published in the *New Yorker*.

John Burnside's *Selected Poems* and a memoir, *A Lie About My Father*, were both published by Cape this year.

Hélène Cixous's ground-breaking essay *The Laugh of the Medusa* (1975) changed the course of feminist philosophy. Recent books available in English include *Stigmata* (1998).

Sarah Corbett's latest collection is *The Witch Bag* (Seren, 2002).

Greg Delanty's *Collected Poems* 1986-2006 is reviewed on pp. 94-5.

Jane Duran's *Coastal* (Enitharmon, 2005) received a PBS Recommendation.

Menna Elfyn's latest collection is *Perfydd Nam* (Perfect Defect) (Gomer).

Bernardine Evaristo's verse novel *Soul Tourists* (Hamish Hamilton) was reviewed in *PR* 95:4.

Allison Funk's latest collection is *The Knot Garden* (Sheep Meadow Press).

Gagan Gill was born in Delhi in 1959. She has published a volume of prose and four collections of poetry.

Kelly Grovier teaches at the University of Wales, Aberystwyth. His first collection, *A Lens in the Palm*, will be published by Carcanet in Autumn 2007.

David Harsent's *Legion* won the 2005 Whitbread Prize for Poetry.

Mohammad Hoghughi, born 1937 in Isfahan, co-founded the literary journal *Jong-e Isfahan*. He has published seven poetry collections, two educational books and six volumes of criticism.

Jane Holland's *The Brief History of a Disreputable Woman* was published by Bloodaxe in 1997. She edits *Poets on Fire*.

Elip ap Hywel's collections are *Ffinau* and *Pethau Brau*.

Andrew Johnston is editor of online poetry resource *The Page*. He has published four collections, most recently *Birds of Europe*.

Parm Kaur's awards including the Saccan Award and a Hawthornden Fellowship. Her chapbook is *Inside the Fourth Dimension* (2003).

Judith Kazantzis's latest collection is *Just After Midnight* (Enitharmon, 2004); more at www.writersartists.net

Mimi Khalvati is the Founder of The Poetry School. Her latest collection is *The Chine* (Carcanet, 2002). She received a 2006 Cholmondeley Award.

John Kinsella's latest books include *The New Arcadia* and *Peripheral Light: New and Selected Poems*, both reviewed in *PR* 96:1.

Satish Kumar is the Editor of *Resurgence* magazine.

Tim Liardet's *The Blood Choir*, reviewed on p. 108, is a PBS recommendation.